SALFORD
AT WORK

PETER HARRIS

AMBERLEY

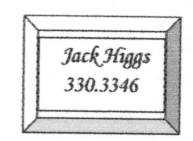

Jack Higgs
330.3346

City of Salford boundary sign. (Courtesy of *Salford Star*)

This book is dedicated to the inventive and industrious people of Salford past and present.

First published 2018

Amberley Publishing
The Hill, Stroud
Gloucestershire, GL5 4EP

www.amberley-books.com

Copyright © Peter Harris, 2018

The right of Peter Harris to be identified as the Author
of this work has been asserted in accordance with the
Copyrights, Designs and Patents Act 1988.

ISBN 978 1 4456 7903 7 (print)
ISBN 978 1 4456 7904 4 (ebook)

British Library Cataloguing in Publication Data.
A catalogue record for this book is available
from the British Library.

Origination by Amberley Publishing.
Printed in the UK.

CONTENTS

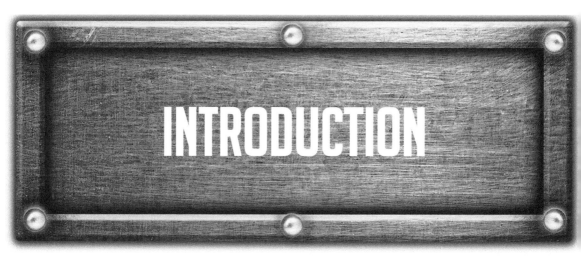

INTRODUCTION

Salford's history, traditions and culture as a place of industry, manufacturing and trade are symbolically and graphically illustrated in the city's coat of arms.

Its long and proud association with the textile industry is depicted by a weaving shuttle surrounded by five worker bees, representing the five original boroughs. Occupying the centre of the shield, a three-masted ship symbolises the major role played by the city's pioneering waterways – the Bridgewater Canal and the Manchester Ship Canal – and flanking it are the iron centres of two millstones, representing the city's rich engineering heritage. Two rampant lions wearing collars of iron and steel further reinforce the city's engineering prowess.

Salford has been a place of work since ancient times, with evidence of human activity dating back 10,000 years to the Stone Age. Neolithic flint arrowheads and tools have been found along the banks of the River Irwell, and during the excavations for the Ship Canal – the 'Big Ditch' as it was known – a Neolithic axe hammer was found near Mode Wheel, the last locks before the former docks.

In the thirteenth century Salford began to take on the character of a small town. In 1228, Henry III granted Salford the right to hold an annual market and fair, and two years later – in

Salford's coat of arms. (Courtesy of Salford City Council)

The Three Crowns. (Courtesy of Sue Richardson)

1230 – the 6th Earl of Chester, Ranulf de Blondeville, granted it a charter, making it a free borough. It set the seal on a period of growth and expansion that would elevate Salford to a position where, for much of its early history, it was more influential and important than its neighbouring big sister, Manchester.

Importantly, too, it was at a Salford pub (The Three Crowns, which stood on Kings Street, Greengate) that in November 1866 an idea blossomed that would have a major impact on the lives of working people across the nation and around the world: the founding of the Trades Union Congress (TUC). Up until then trade unions, societies and councils existed in isolation, largely ignored and their members often exploited, but after the enlightened group of trade unionists met at the Salford pub all would change. The group's president, Samuel Nicholson, put forward the concept of a 'congress of our own' and a little over twelve months later trade unions from all over the UK came to Manchester, where the first Trades Union Congress was held at the Mechanics' Institute. Salford had sparked off a movement that would bring tangible benefits to working men and women the world over.

Salford takes its name from the Old English word *sealhford*, literally 'a ford by the willow trees' (*salix* in Latin) that grew along the banks of the River Irwell, which today can still be seen in the Lower Broughton area. This bucolic imagery belies, however, the true gritty nature of a city that until its twenty-first-century reincarnation was characterised by the chimney-stacked mills and cloth-capped workers depicted by artist L. S. Lowry and the cobbles of *Coronation Street* created by the Salfordian Tony Warren.

Today, Salford is, in reality, a tale of two cities. In one, vestiges of the old city can still be seen, often in the form of listed mills and breweries now given a new lease of life as smart business villages.

Above: Going to Work by L. S. Lowry, 1959. (Courtesy of The Lowry Centre)

Left: Self Portrait by L. S. Lowry. (Courtesy of The Lowry Centre)

Alongside is the gleaming high-tech metropolis of Salford Quays and MediaCityUK, which continues to expand on what was the derelict wasteland of Salford Docks. Salford was granted city status in 1926 and less than 100 years later it was heralded as the number one destination in the UK for start-up businesses, outranking both London and Manchester. There are now more than 10,500 businesses of all kinds in Salford, with a total workforce of 121,000 employees.

MILLS, MACHINES AND MARKETS

Just a few years before the start of the Industrial Revolution, maps and prints published by Casson and Berry in 1751 show Salford as little more than a village with a church towering over a cluster of buildings surrounded by fields, but it was a landscape soon to change.

In 1758, the first steamboat in the world was built in Worsley by Salford engineers Messrs Sharratt, and a year later the 3rd Duke of Bridgewater commissioned Derbyshire engineer James Brindley to build the country's first major canal to transport coal from his mines in Worsley to Manchester. When the Bridgewater Canal opened in 1761 it was in many ways the spark that ignited the Industrial Revolution and the reign of King Cotton in Salford, along with the rest of Lancashire.

Even before the Industrial Revolution, however, and the introduction of cotton, Salford had a tradition of textile production and processing with a brisk trade in woollen goods and thick, hard-wearing twills or fustians, often used for labourers and worn by prisoners. Clog making, cobbling, weaving and brewing were among other prevalent cottage industries.

Salford's damp climate (which made cotton threads less likely to snap) and the abundant supply of water from the River Irwell made it fertile territory in which the new industrial age could prosper, and from the 1860s huge monolithic textile mills, as well as engineering factories and iron foundries, began to change the skyline.

The South West Prospect of Manchester and Salford by Robert Whitworth, printer and bookseller, 1834. (Courtesy of Chetham Library)

Above: Bridgewater Canal, *c.* 1910–20. (Courtesy of Peel Group Archives)

Below: Bridgewater Canal, Patricroft, 1934. (Courtesy of Peel Group Archives)

Francis Egerton, 3rd Duke of
Bridgewater. (Courtesy of Peel
Group Archives)

Apart from cotton spinning, the industry gave rise to all manner of specialist processes and practices, and with it a whole new language. There were bleachers, dyers, calenderers, printers, finishers, sizers, stretchers, embossers, perchers, moranders, winders, warpers and many more. Silk spinning also flourished alongside cotton and other mills specialised in the production of plush, velvet, flax, lint, gingham and the so-called small ware (including labels, coat loops, mantles and linen goods).

In tandem with the textile explosion Salford also witnessed an exponential rise in the number of engineering companies, with many producing bespoke machines to support the textile industry but also a vast range of innovative machines and equipment, including steam engines, hydraulic pumps, cranes, fire engines, gears and pumps, washing and laundry equipment, weighing machines, factory clocks, screws and bolts, turnstiles, lathes, and even mangles. Much of this pioneering hardware found a resting place for posterity in museums of science and industry, but examples of Salford's industrial flair and prowess can still be seen all over Britain and in many parts of the world – as far away as Egypt, India and New Zealand.

For the best part of 200 years the textile industry, coupled with engineering, were the dominant forces in Salford. Some of the most notable mills are given in the following section.

PHILLIPS & LEE

In 1805, the Salford Cotton Mill, otherwise known as Phillips & Lee, was the first industrialised mill in the world to be illuminated by gas – some four years after Scottish engineer and inventor William Murdoch first conceived the idea. At first just fifty gaslights flickered in the gloom, but quickly this increased to more than 900. Progress, at first, was slow, with the need to overcome several practical problems such as removing the smell of the gas by purifying it with lime and finding the optimum temperature to heat the coal to obtain the maximum quantity of gas.

Left: William Murdoch, 1839. (Courtesy of Grace's Guide to British Industrial History)

Below: Lowry Mill, Swinton, originally Newtown Mill, built in 1883. (Courtesy of Lowry Mill)

NEWTOWN MILL (NOW LOWRY MILL)

Built in 1883, the former five-storey cotton-spinning mill in Swinton, Newtown Mill, which served the industry for more than 100 years, is one of only a handful still standing. It was renamed the Lowry Mill in 2008 in deference to the Salford artist L. S. Lowry, who lived close by at No. 117 Station Road for thirty-six years, visiting on several occasions in his day job capacity as a rent collector.

Operated originally by John Knowles & Sons, the mill rattled to the sound of **83,000** spindles and was one of the region's biggest employers in its heyday. Having been owned by

Restaurant area in the new Lowry Mill. (Courtesy of Lowry Mill)

the Lancashire Cotton Corporation, it was occupied by the Dorma Group from 1963 to 2008 (a division of Coats Viyella plc), manufacturing household linen and soft furnishings.

Now, having been acquired by Vanguard Holdings and having undergone a £12 million refurbishment, it has been given a new lease of life as luxury offices, complete with an on-site restaurant, gym and meeting facilities.

ISLINGTON MILL

One of the world's first steam-powered 'fireproof' mills, Islington Mill at Ordsall was built in 1823 for cotton spinner and engineer Nathan Gough by architect David Bellhouse, who was also responsible for Manchester's original Town Hall and the city's Portico Library.

Gough was an ingenious, self-educated man, who in 1929, according to a report in the respected *Manchester Guardian*, 'made his appearance in the streets at Manchester, steering his new steam-carriage, which appeared to move at the rate of six or seven miles an hour'. It was 'followed by immense crowds of people who seemed very much pleased with the treat of riding upon this novel conveyance'. He died in 1852, aged sixty-two.

The original mill suffered a partial collapse, in which nineteen workers lost their lives. When it was rebuilt, a single row of cast-iron columns was added to reinforce the structure, an innovation thought to have influenced the designs of the first New York skyscrapers.

Along with the renamed Lowry, the Grade II-listed Islington Mill is one of few remaining in Salford, albeit with an entirely different purpose. Since 2000, it has been the home of the Islington Arts Club – a vibrant, creative space and arts hub with galleries, studios, a public visual-and-music arts event programme and its own bed and breakfast accommodation. Some fifty-plus businesses and more than 100 artists call the mill home.

Islington Mill, Ordsall, built in 1823. (Courtesy of Grace's Guide to British Industrial History)

ORDSALL DYE WORKS

In 1837, on the retirement of their wealthy father, James Worrall and John Mayo Worrall became the third generation to run the business since its foundation in 1786, proudly advertising it as 'Velveteen Dyers to the World'. They soon began a programme of takeovers, acquiring several companies in Lancashire and Yorkshire. At the peak of its production, the huge Ordsall Dye Works had a workforce of around 3,000. At both the Franco-British Exhibition in 1908 and the Turin Exhibition in 1911, they won the Grand Prix.

J. & J. M. WORRALL
LIMITED.
Premier Velveteen Dyers of the World.

Established over 150 years ago.

DYERS, PRINTERS, EMBOSSERS AND FINISHERS OF VELVETEENS, Cords, Moles, Twills, &c.

Specialists in the Dyeing and Finishing of Fast Dyed Velveteens.

PURCHASERS SHOULD SECURE WORRALL'S FAST-TO-RUBBING VELVETEENS, CHIFFON FINISH.

ORDSALL DYE WORKS, SALFORD, MANCHESTER.

An Ordsall Dye Work advertisement. (Courtesy of Grace's Guide to British Industrial History)

The height of fashion – a Reville creation in Worrall-dyed velveteen. (Courtesy of Grace's Guide to British Industrial History)

A *Reville* Creation in WORRALL DYED VELVET

In 1890 it became a private limited company and remained so until 1899 when it joined forces with other similar companies to form the English Velvet & Cord Dyers Association, which was shortened to English Velvets in 1948. The Ordsall premises closed in 1964.

MONTON MILL

Situated on the Bridgewater Canal in the parish of Eccles, the Monton cotton-spinning mill was built in 1906, becoming one of the biggest employers in the area and dominating the surrounding skyline. It had more than 91,000 mule spindles and most of its textile machinery was supplied by Platt Brothers & Co. of Oldham, one of the leading engineering companies at the time.

In 1930, the mill was taken over by the Lancashire Cotton Corporation and in 1964 it became a part of the giant Courtaulds Group. Production eventually came to an end and

Monton Mill, built in 1906. (Courtesy of Grace's Guide to British Industrial History)

an important part of Salford's industrial heritage was erased for good when the building was demolished, its massive chimney razed to the ground by celebrity steeplejack the late Fred Dibnah.

OTHER SALFORD NOTABLES

Some of Salford's mills have gained a place in history for other reasons. In November 1915, the *Salford City Reporter* reported that thirty-six-year-old Frank Howarth, the third son of millionaire mill owner George Howarth, was shot and killed by a German sniper while serving during the First World War in France. Howarth Mill, also known as Ordsall Mills and simply as 'Dickie Howarth's', was opened in 1872 and at its height employed 4,000 workers, mostly women and girls working in weaving sheds across Salford.

The Acme Mill at Pendlebury, built in 1905, was the first Lancashire mill to be driven solely by electricity, but it is now best known as the subject of the 1930 painting by L. S. Lowry *Coming from the Mill*.

One of Salford's most imposing mills was built in 1906 at Canalside, Winton, for the Eccles Spinning & Manufacturing Co. to replace two other mills in the area that had been destroyed in fires with major job losses. As recently as 2013 it was demolished.

The Adelphi area of Salford, alongside the distinctive U-bend in the River Irwell and close to the elegant former residential areas of the Crescent, was home to the Adelphi Dye Works from the 1830s, an extensive industrial complex engaged in textile processing – principally bleaching, sizing, dyeing and printing. The Adelphi Print Works, the Adelphi Logwood Mills and former Adelphi Baths were other well-known landmarks in the vicinity.

Coming from the Mill by L. S. Lowry, 1930. (Courtesy The Lowry Centre)

ENGINEERING

For the best part of 150 years, with the Industrial Revolution at its core, Salford was one of the great northern engineering powerhouses, producing a miscellany of ingenious machines that revolutionised manufacturing processes throughout Britain and were exported to all corners of the globe.

Many of them, proving that necessity is, indeed, the mother of invention, were bespoke machines and devices facilitating the various facets of the cotton and textile manufacturing, but still more provided the hardware and power that fuelled every conceivable kind of industry at home and overseas. Inside the proliferation of Salford factories, workers were producing gas and steam engines, cranes, firefighting equipment, pumps, lathes, seals, weighing machines, turnstiles, industrial clocks, switchgears, brick- and tile-making equipment, railway equipment and much more.

One of the earliest and most diverse engineering companies was W. H. Bailey & Co., established by John Bailey at Salford's Albion Works in 1839. By the turn of the century their production portfolio included turret clocks, steam and water gauges, pumps and valves, barometers, tide recorders, gas jet motors, turnstiles, lightning conductors, lifts, hoists and

'Over the Tomb of the Prophet' – one of Bailey's turret clocks. (Courtesy of Grace's Guide to British Industrial History)

A Bailey turnstile made at the Albion Works, Salford. (Courtesy of Grace's Guide to British Industrial History)

motors for the wire-rope haulage of trucks on mountain railways. In 1999 they acquired a foundry in Salford to produce motor car engines, and in 1908 the company won awards at the Franco-British Exhibition for its steam engines and for carriage building.

Established around 1841, Ellis & Noton, ironfounders, millwrights, engineers and machine makers of the Irwell Foundry in Stanley Street, Salford, were also among the early pioneers. In 1844, they produced the Ellis Turntable, a 'stupendous piece of machinery' that revolutionised the method of constructing railway turntables, greatly reducing the wear and tear on both the turntable and the rail carriages passing over them. It also doubled as a weighing machine. They were used on many of the major rail links between the great northern cities as well as in Ireland. An associate company – H. & J. Ellis, also of the Irwell Foundry – manufactured a vast range of engineering and machine tools including massive overhead steam-driven cranes and jib cranes, one of which is still believed to have survived in Tarle, South Australia.

Another Salford crane maker F. Taylor & Sons (founded in 1895 in Bolton Road, Pendleton) was the first company in the world to produce cranes using a slewing jib with hydraulics. They were best known, however, for their snoop-nosed crane, known as the Jumbo, which was in service at Manchester Airport for a time.

Several Salford engineering firms received orders for their goods from all corners of the globe. Sir James Farmer & Sons of the Adelphi Iron Works supplied a new ironwork to the King of Burma to be located on the Irrawaddy River, around 12 miles from Mandalay. It included blast-furnace engines, hoists for a wire-drawing and rail-straightening machine and a tube-making plant. Their specialities included machinery for bleaching, dyeing and finishing cotton goods and linoleum and floor cloth machines.

In 1862, two powerful steam engines for use in the cotton industry, made by Routledge & Ommanney of the New Bridge Foundry in Adelphi Street, Salford, were shipped out to Egypt to be used near Alexandria in the preparation of Egyptian cotton. Before leaving, it was reported that 'they were examined by several scientific gentlemen and photographs taken

An Ellis & Noton jib crane. (Courtesy of Grace's Guide to British Industrial History)

Made in Salford – a Taylor Jumbo crane. (Courtesy of Grace's Guide to British Industrial History)

of them'. A cotton factory at Zifta (sometimes Zefta) on the River Nile in Egypt was also the destination for an engine, gearing equipment and two boilers supplied by Gadd & Hull of the Regent Works, Salford, in 1863. In 1875, Deakin, Parker & Co., engineers based at the Sandon Works in Salford, made a horizontal compound steam engine for Manchester Corporation's Water Street Works and another, of precisely the same design, for the Turkish government. Another similar horizontal steam engine, constructed by Hamilton Wood & Co. at the Liver Iron Foundry on the banks of the Irwell, was delivered in 1869 to drive machinery at the workshops of the Tasmania Railways.

Founded in 1850, Thomas Bradford of the Crescent Iron Works, Salford, were among the country's leading 'laundry, dairy, domestic, bath and cooking engineers'. Among their many products were a combined washing, mangling and wringing machine, the quaintly named Ye Tudor castellated mangle and a range of laundry items – and also a butter churn – that ended their days in the Falkland Islands.

ROUTLEDGE AND OMMANNEY,

ENGINEERS, ADELPHI STREET, SALFORD, MANCHESTER,

MAKERS OF

PUMPING ENGINES FOR MINES, WATERWORKS, IRRIGATION :

ALSO AMMONIA PUMPS FOR GASWORKS, &c.

HIGH PRESSURE AND CONDENSING ENGINES.

AIR COMPRESSING ENGINES.

Hydraulic Packing Press for cloths, yarns, COTTON, hay, jute, &c.

Cotton Seed Hullers.

Water-Power Engines and Pumps, [driven by water power, on Messrs. Lonsdale and Peete's patent.

R. and O.'s Improved Steam and Water Valves and Taps, in Brass and Iron.

R. and O.'s Improved Hand Fire Engines.

Brass Bowls, Gun-metal Working Barrels, and other heavy Gun-metal Castings.

BABBITS' & DEWRANCE'S PATENT METALS

Stores for M'Neill's Boiler and Roofing Felt.

R. and O's Direct Double-Acting Pumping Engines,
Constructed from 2in. up to 18in. diameter, have been many years used for Water-works, Forcing Water out of Mines, Irrigation, Stationary Fire Engines, and Feeding Boilers. They are simple in construction and reliable. 0578

Above: Routledge & Ommanney advertisement for double-action pumping engine. (Courtesy of Grace's Guide to British Industrial History)

Below: Deakin, Parker & Co. advertisement for double-action condenser. (Courtesy of Grace's Guide to British Industrial History)

DOUBLE-ACTING CONDENSERS

OF IMPROVED DESIGN.

For attaching to new or old steam engines, effecting a power or fuel economy of 20 to 30 per cent. Ample capacity and thorough accessibility.

PRICES.

Diameter of Engine Cylinder	in. 9	in. 10	in. 12	in. 14	in. 16	in. 18	in. 20	in. 22	in. 24	in. 26	in. 30
Price of suitable condenser, fitted with brass piston and ring, brass covered air pump, rod, and all fittings	£ 40	£ 45	£ 50	£ 60	£ 65	£ 70	£ 80	£ 85	£ 95	£ 100	£ 120

STATIONARY

Steam Engines,

1 TO 100-H.P.

Condensing, Non-Condensing, and Compound.

First Prize Medals, Manchester Exhibitions, 1874 & '75.

THE HIGHEST CLASS OF WORK GUARANTEED.

DEAKIN, PARKER, & CO., Sandon Works, Salford, MANCHESTER.

Proprietors: T. BROWETT & H. LINDLEY

(LATE OF SIR J. WHITWORTH & CO., LIMITED).

A major contribution to the Age of Steam was made De Bergue & Co., of the Strangeways Ironworks in Salford. In the 1850s the firm began by manufacturing vulcanised rubber, as well as buffers and bearing springs for railway and other carriages. In 1871 they were awarded the contract to build the original Tay Bridge and set up a dedicated factory at the small town of Wormit on the Firth of Tay. In 1888 they patented a 'simple, handy and powerful' hand-held device for lifting railway lines that was described as 'indispensable for stations, crowded sidings and tunnels'.

Established in 1868, with premises at the Bridgewater Street Iron Works in Salford, electric cable maker Walter Glover & Co. went on to become contractors to HM Postmaster General, the Indian government and a supplier to all the major rail, telephone and electric light companies. In addition to a wide range of covered wires, aerial lines, electric light leads and cables, they had a fascinating sideline in making cotton-covered wire for use in crinolines and for covering hair curlers. They exported across Europe, including Norway and Sweden.

Another major firm of electric engineers, Dorman & Smith, traded from the Ordsall Electrical Works in Salford from 1894, manufacturing switchgear, fuse boards, circuit breakers, ceiling plates, and wall sockets as well as lamp holders and shades for leading contractors across the UK and in 'the colonies and abroad'.

Weighbridge and weighing machine manufacturers Hodgson & Stead operated from two sites in Salford, the Egerton Works in Irwell Street and the Hope Foundry in Sandon Street. Founded in 1852, they supplied collieries, blast furnaces, iron forges, rolling mills, markets, warehouses, paper makers, cotton and wool mills as well as road and rail constructors. They also made cranes and turntables.

As makers of 'anything and everything' for firefighting, including fire engines, hose couplings and fire extinguishers, John Morris & Sons made their first commercial vehicle in 1906, moving

Above: A Thomas Bradford multipurpose mangle. (Courtesy of Grace's Guide to British Industrial History)

Right: Advertisement for de Bergue's Rail Lifter. (Courtesy of Grace's Guide to British Industrial History)

Maintenance of Permanent Way.
THE
RAIL LIFTER.
Simple,
Handy, Powerful.

Indispensable for Stations, Crowded Sidings. and Tunnels.

Do Bergue's Patent Improved
RAIL LIFTER.
For Particulars and Price apply to   7141
DE BERGUE & CO.,
LIMITED,
Strangeways Ironworks. MANCHESTER.

MANUFACTURERS (by Patent Processes) of Silk and Cotton Covered Wire and Tape of all Sizes for Electrical Purposes. Cables and Multiple Wire for the various Systems. Elegant Designs in Silk Covered Flexible Wire for Lamp Suspending, &c. Double Concentric Electric Light Cables for Ship Work. Aërial and Underground Cables to any Specification. Special Anti-Induction Cables for the Telephone.

Telegram Address—" WALTER GLOVER, SALFORD."   *London Address—10, HATTON GARDEN, E.C.*

SALFORD, MANCHESTER.

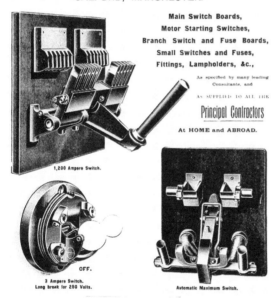

DORMAN & SMITH,

SALFORD, MANCHESTER.

**Main Switch Boards,
Motor Starting Switches,
Branch Switch and Fuse Boards,
Small Switches and Fuses,
Fittings, Lampholders, &c.,**

As specified by many leading
Consultants, and

As SUPPLIED TO ALL THE

Principal Contractors

At HOME and ABROAD.

1,200 Ampere Switch.

*3 Ampere Switch.
Long break for 250 Volts.*

OFF.

Automatic Maximum Switch.

Above: Glover's advertisement for leads and cables. (Courtesy of Grace's Guide to British Industrial History)

Left: Dorman & Smith's traction switchboard. (Courtesy of Grace's Guide to British Industrial History)

FIRST-HAND MANUFACTURERS OF

CONTROLLING APPARATUS AND ACCESSORIES FOR

ELECTRIC LIGHT & POWER PLANTS,

TRACTION SWITCHBOARDS.

into the Salford Fire Engine Works three years later. One of their first engines is in the National Rail Museum in Delhi, India. The company, which also made steam motor wagons, tractors and ploughs, ceased vehicle production in 1921.

Machinery for rock drilling, as well as various forms of engines and compressors, was made by Thomas Larmuth & Co. of the Todleben Works, close to the old Salford cattle market. The company started out as chain makers in Salford in the 1850s. Brailey & Co., founded

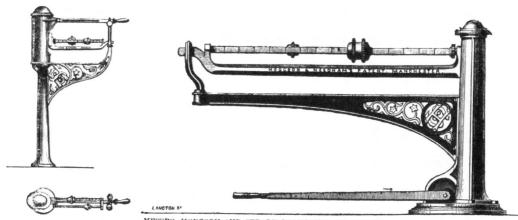

MESSRS. HODGSON AND STEAD'S POLYGONAL STEELYARD.

Above: Hodgson & Stead's weighing equipment. (Courtesy of Grace's Guide to British Industrial History)

Right: Now a museum exhibit – a John Morris fire engine. (Courtesy of Grace's Guide to British Industrial History)

in Salford's Spaw Street in 1890, specialised in electroplating and by 1939 were offering an anodising service 'for all aircraft finishes'. John Cameron, another big Salford company formed in 1870, operated from the Oldfield Road Ironworks in 1880 making steam-driven pumps and punching and shearing machines, many of which can now be seen in museums of industry. Another Salford company, G. Birch & Co., which dates back to the 1890s, manufactured high-quality lathes, planing, milling, drilling and cutting machines at the Islington Tool Works in Salford. They even had a special plant for making wire mattresses. Around the same time, Cunliffe & Croom were making similar machines at the Broughton Iron Works, and even earlier – from 1869 – Lowry & Co. of Cross Street, Salford, were producing screw-cutting equipment and lathes as well as fans, grindstones and special machines for processing flax, hemp and jute. It has not been established if the company had any familial links with the artist L. S. Lowry.

Several other non-engineering Salford firms and businesses, spanning more than a century and a half, are also worthy of note. Atkinson & Barker of Greengate, Salford (established 1847), were chemists by Special Appointment to Her Majesty Queen Victoria. In bottles costing from

THESE NEED **CHROMIUM—HARD**

- BRAKES
- SPRINGS
- ENGINE
- STEERING

The treatment of shackle pins, king pins, fulcrum pins, pivot pins, etc., with hard chromium deposition is a process specification insisted upon by the leading heavy vehicle manufacturers. Hard chromium ensures long life and gives the benefit of the anti-seize properties of chromium.

BRAILEY

BRAILEY ELECTROPLATERS LTD.
CHAPEL ST · SALFORD 3 · M/C

Left: Advertisement for chromium electroplating by Brailey's of Salford. (Courtesy of Grace's Guide to British Industrial History)

Below: An advertisement for a Cunliffe & Croom disc-grinding machine made at the Broughton Iron Works in Salford. (Courtesy of Graces's Guide to British Industrial History)

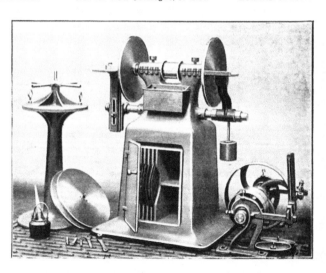

CUNLIFFE & CROOM, LTD.,

BROUGHTON IRON WORKS, MANCHESTER.

Telegrams—"Lathe, Manchester."   Ask for New Catalogue, or List.   Established 1864.

DISC GRINDER.

Grinds Hardened or Mild Metals.

Good Work quickly & accurately produced.

Samples sent to us will be ground to show accuracy & quality of finish, & time occupied stated.

Reasonable price.

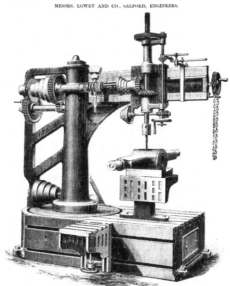

IMPROVED DRILLING AND SLOTTING MACHINE.

MESSRS. LOWRY AND CO., SALFORD, ENGINEERS.

Right: One of Lowry & Co.'s drilling and slotting machines. (Courtesy of Grace's Guide to British Industrial History)

Below: An advertisement for children's medicine by Atkinson & Barker's, chemists by royal appointment to Queen Victoria. (Courtesy of Grace's Guide to British Industrial History)

ATKINSON & BARKER'S
CELEBRATED ROYAL INFANTS' PRESERVATIVE,

SO RENOWNED FOR ITS EFFICACY IN

Preventing or removing the Disorders to which infancy is the most peculiarly liable, as *Convulsions, Gripes, Tooth Fever, Rickets, Measles, Hooping Cough*, &c. is Prepared and Sold, Wholesale and Retail (under the License and Authority of his Assignees), by

34, Greengate, Salford,

Chemist, by Special Appointment, to Her Most Gracious Majesty Queen Victoria.

In Bottles, at 1*s.* 1½*d.*, 2*s.* 9*d.*, and 4*s.* 6*d.* each.

1 old shilling and 1 and a half pence, they produced a 'Celebrated Royal Infants' Preventative' for disorders of infancy including 'convulsions, gripe, tooth fever, rickets, measles and hooping cough' – spelled then without the initial 'w'.

A year later, in 1848, a Mrs Lough advertised the opening of her Peel Park Refreshment House in Salford offering the 'nobility, clergy, gentry and commercial and working classes' a 'commodious refreshment house' offering cakes, confectionery, ices, creams, jellies and British wine along with a selection of ginger beers, lemonade, seltzer water and fruit juices. During the park opening hours, hot and cold baths and showers were also available.

One hundred later, P. Webber, who set up in business in Hayfield Mills, Percy Street, Pendleton in 1941, was making a range of celluloid-skin dressed dolls with names such as

PEEL PARK
REFRESHMENT HOUSE,
SALFORD.
MRS. LOUGH

Begs respectfully to announce to the Nobility, Clergy, Gentry, and Commercial and Working Classes generally, that she has entered upon the above commodious REFRESHMENT HOUSE, and hopes by strict attention to the comfort and convenience of the Visiters to the Park, to merit their liberal support and patronage.

Mrs. Lough has made the necessary arrangements for accommodating SCHOOLS, WEDDING, PIC NIC, and other PRIVATE PARTIES with VIANDS of the best description, and on the most reasonable terms.

A spacious Room is appropriated exclusively for MORNING CONCERTS, LECTURES and LITERARY and SCIENTIFIC MEETINGS.

Mrs. Lough having engaged a first-rate Confectioner will be enabled to supply Families and Visiters with every description of CAKES and CONFECTIONERY, ICES, CREAMS, JELLIES, &c. BRITISH WINES (which are exhilarating without being intoxicating). SLUGG'S celebrated Ginger Beer, Lemonade, Soda and Carrara Waters always on hand. The pure SELTZER WATER, Bottled and Capsuled at the Spring. HAWKINS' distinguished Beverages, viz:—Original Vauxhall Sherbet, London Champagne, Ginger Beer, Raspberry, Aerated Beer, Le Beverage D'Orange; Raspberry, Orange, Green and Lemon Gingerettes and concentrated Lemonade.

Mrs. Lough has also the pleasure to announce that a Room will shortly be Opened for BILLIARDS, a New Table of the best description being now in progress for this Establishment.

N.B.—*Hot, Cold and Shower BATHS, during the time the Park is open.*

☞ An OMNIBUS passes the Park Gate between MANCHESTER and PENDLETON *every quarter of an hour*; the Park being only five minutes drive from the Manchester Exchange.

PEEL PARK REFRESHMENT HOUSE, *Salford, June,* 1848.

Mrs Lough promotes her Salford Refreshment House. (Courtesy of Grace's Guide to British Industrial History)

PICNIC TRAYS

The Crowning Comfort and Utility for Motorists

THE "E.C. FIX" MOTOR TRAY

A long-felt want supplied. Ideal for alfresco meals and scores of other uses. Simply hooks on the back of the seats by means of "Patent Spring Clips," holding the tray in position without damage to the upholstery.

ALL BRITISH! MADE IN OAK! (MAHOGANY 1/- EACH EXTRA).

TO FIT ANY CAR. ALWAYS HANDY— NEVER IN THE WAY.

Popular Sizes 14″ × 7″	Price 6/6 each
" 14″ × 9″	7/- "
Austin 7 and Morris 8, 12″ × 8″	6/6 "
Bench Seats, thick upholstery, 18″ × 9″	9/- "
Window Trays, 14″ × 6″. Fit inside or outside.	
For driver's use and front seat passengers	6/6 "

(Packed in cartons)

OBTAINABLE FROM: The Motor Dept. of Whiteley's, Ltd., London; Gamages, Holborn; Army and Navy Stores, Victoria Street, London; Harrods Ltd.; Benetfinks, Cheapside, London; Selfridges, London; Boots Cash Chemists (Fancy Goods Dept.), Royal Exchange, Manchester, and Branches; Beales Ltd., Bournemouth; James Grose Ltd., 379 Euston Road, London, N.W.1; and other leading stores.

If unobtainable, direct from the Manufacturers (C.O.D.):

STANIHURST WORKS LTD., 56 Liverpool Street, Salford, 5, Lancs.

Above: Stanihurst's Salford-made E. C. Fix motor tray. (Courtesy of Grace's Guide to British Industrial History)

Left: Sleepy and Mama – two of the dolls made by Webber in Salford. (Courtesy of Grace's Guide to British Industrial History)

Advertisement for Pochin's clay. (Courtesy of Grace's Guide to British Industrial History)

Mama and Sleepy Eyes. They also produced toys, baby rattles, tables lamps, candle shades and bed lamps. Around the same time, the Stanihurst Works in Liverpool Street, Salford, were producing the innovative E. C. Fix picnic motor tray, which could be hooked onto the back of car seats. They were sold for 6s 6d (1s extra for a mahogany tray) at Selfridges, Boots, Gamages and the Army and Navy stores.

Two other fascinating Salford companies were H. D. Pochin, clay producers of Worsley Street and J. D. Mansergh & Son of the Wheathill Charcoal Works. In the mid-nineteenth century Henry Davis Pochin invented a process to make a low-cost alternative to alum stone in the production of alum cake used in paper manufacture and to service the business he bought several china clay mines in Cornwall becoming one of the country's three largest producers of china clay. Established in 1781, Mansergh made coal dust, coke dust, pure oak charcoal and mineral blacking.

MARKETS

The sight of a cow plodding its way over the main thoroughfare of Cross Lane would certainly bring the traffic to a halt if it were to happen today, but for almost 100 years it would have been a common, if somewhat incongruous, occurrence.

Victorian Salford was not blessed with rolling verdant pastures grazed by herds of contented cattle, but in July 1837 a cattle market was opened in Cross Lane near to the junction with Broad Street, which reputedly became the second largest sheep and cattle market of its kind in the country, with six slaughterhouses and even its own bank.

Cattle being driven across Cross Lane, with Cattle Market Hotel in the background. (Courtesy of Salford Local History Library Collection)

Salford's once-flourishing cattle market. (Courtesy of Salford Local History Library Collection)

For two days in 1872 (12–14 December) it held what was known as the Fat Cattle Show. After a period of eighteen years, it was resurrected and held for a second time on 12 December 1910. Two outbreaks of foot-and-mouth disease closed the market in February 1922 and again in March 1924. On 31 March 1931, after trading for almost sixty years, the cattle market closed for good.

After some years, the site of the former cow and sheep pens was converted into the legendary Cross Lane open-air street market, with larger-than-life stallholders selling everything from clothing to crockery, carpets to curtains. It was a Salford institution beloved by the local population, but in 2011 a decision was taken to close it when civic leaders became aware that its stalls had been infiltrated by traders dealing in counterfeit goods.

THE 'BIG DITCH' AND THE DOCKS

Salford's contribution to the Industrial Revolution was given a major boost in 1894 with the opening of the Manchester Ship Canal and an extensive system of docks mostly within the Salford boundaries.

The 36-mile-long canal – or the 'Big Ditch' as it was often affectionately called – was an iconic and audacious feat of engineering, arguably the greatest of the Victorian era. Almost overnight, Salford and Manchester became Britain's third busiest ports, literally bringing about a sea-change stimulus to the region's economy. Not only did the docks greatly enhance the fortunes of established businesses with opportunities to develop overseas markets, they also became a new and expanding workplace in their own right.

Salford was at the hub of the Industrial Revolution and the opening of waterway to the sea was fortuitously timely. It provided a transportation artery to and from the rest of the world, importantly at a time when trade and industry was being hit by cripplingly high transport charges by the railway companies and the Liverpool Dock Board. At its peak, Salford Docks

Construction work on the Manchester Ship Canal – the 'Big Ditch' – 1890. (Courtesy of Salford Local History Library Collection)

A 'Coffee Man' providing hot drinks for the canal's construction workers. (Courtesy of Salford Local History Library Collection)

Canal navvies and soil transporter, c. 1890. (Courtesy of Peel Group Archives)

(or Manchester Docks as it was also known) was handling 10 per cent of the country's import and export trade with as many as 5,000 ships entering the port every year.

Vessels weighing up to 12,500 tonnes arrived with raw cotton, cars, grain, timber, tea, fruit, lard, oil and petroleum as well as frozen meat. Exports included the finished cotton products and textiles as well as locomotives and heavy-duty machines such as turbines and hydraulic pumps that dramatically improved the lifestyle of the populations in developing countries. To lift the goods on and off the ships, there were some 200 cranes.

In its heyday around 5,000 people worked on the docks as stevedores or general labourers, a high proportion of them living in the surrounding Salford districts of Ordsall, Weaste and Pendleton. The work, especially in the depths of winter, was gruelling and sometimes fraught with danger. Salfordians who remember the docks in its post-war years often refer to it as the 'Barbary Coast', with suggestions of press-gang activity in some of the area's rough dockland pubs.

After a three-year struggle to overcome considerable opposition and scepticism, work finally started on the canal on 11 November 1887 when the first sod of earth was cut in a field in the River Mersey estuary, later to become Eastham Locks. Giant mechanical excavators were shortly brought into use, but much of the work still required the muscle-power of an

Dockers unloading bananas from waggons, *c.* 1911. (Courtesy of Peel Group Archives)

Street decorations for the official canal opening by Queen Victoria, 1894. (Courtesy of Salford Local History Library Collection)

army of 16,000 navvies using picks, spades and wheelbarrows. Hundreds more bricklayers, carpenters, stonemasons and other artisans were also permanently employed on the project.

Several major difficulties – including the death of the contractor, flooding and cash problems – threatened to jeopardise the undertaking, but all were eventually resolved and by November 1893 the Manchester Ship Canal was a navigable waterway. To mark its commercial opening on New Year's Day 1894, a flotilla of seventy-one ships led by the steam yacht *The Norseman* (owned by ardent supporter Samuel Platt and with the canal company directors on board) sailed into the Salford terminal from Latchford in Warrington, passing through the Barton Swing Aqueduct. It was followed by *Snowdrop*, carrying members of the council. *The Pioneer*, a steamer owned by the Co-operative Wholesale Society, was given the honour of unloading the first cargo.

Above: A painting of the *Norseman* leading the opening processions through the Barton Swing Aqueduct en route for the docks followed by *The Snowdrop*, 1 January 1894. (Courtesy of Salford Local History Library Collection)

Below: One of the Manchester Liners, the *Frontier*, passing under the Latchford Viaduct. (Courtesy of the Captain Eric Askew collection)

Four months later, on 21 May, the streets around the docks entrance were bedecked with flags and bunting, and a massive crowd gathered to greet Queen Victoria as she arrived to perform the official opening ceremony by pulling a cord from her seat aboard the royal yacht, *The Enchantress*.

In 1898, more than ten years after its opening, Salford Docks became the home of Manchester Liners, the passenger and cargo shipping line that plied its trade across the Atlantic and parts of the Mediterranean. In December 1969, a five-storey glass-fronted building with a curved façade was opened as the company's headquarters: Manchester Liners House.

The *Manchester Renown* navigates the Ship Canal. (Courtesy of Eric Slavin)

The *Dorothea* from Limassol, Cyprus, docked in Salford. (Courtesy of Peel Group Archives)

SALFORD'S INDUSTRIAL GIANTS

O ver the centuries Salford has spawned many of the country's biggest and most influential companies, several of them now in their prime and continuing to expand. Among them are a number of classic rags-to-riches stories where hard work, perseverance and entrepreneurial acumen have overcome adversity and poverty to reap rich dividends. Below are some of Salford's division-one players.

MATHER & PLATT

From its humble beginnings in 1834 in Brown Street, conveniently close to the River Irwell, Mather & Platt became a global leader in the design and manufacture of high-quality engineered products and systems that improved living standards worldwide.

The Isle of Man's electric tram built by Mather and Platt, 1898. (Courtesy of Grace's Guide to British Industrial History)

COMPLETE EQUIPMENTS FOR

ELECTRIC RAILWAYS AND ELECTRIC TRAMWAYS

SUPPLIED BY

MATHER & PLATT, LTD., Mechanical, Electrical and Hydraulic Engineers.

SALFORD IRON WORKS, MANCHESTER.

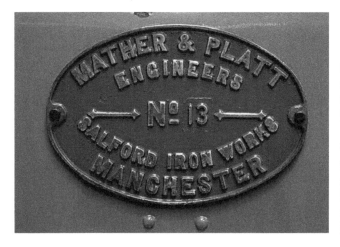

Left: A Mather & Platt rail carriage sign. (Courtesy of Grace's Guide to British Industrial History)

Below: Motor and trailer car on the Douglas & Laxey electric railway built by Mather & Platt. (Courtesy of Grace's Guide to British Industrial History)

It was there where Colin Mather (also known as Peter Colin Mather), a Scotsman who was registered as a cabinetmaker in Gun Street in 1817, made the transition to machine making and started a business empire that was to embrace textile machinery, pumps, submarine motors and electricity generators.

Initially, 'Cast-Iron Colin', as he came to be known, and his brother William described themselves as 'engineers, machine makers and millwrights' making good-quality rollers and sundry equipment for the local textile bleaching industry. In 1845, for reasons that remain obscure, the Mathers formed an association with John Platt, a machine maker living at Roman Road terrace, Higher Broughton in Salford who leased them part of the Salford Iron Works – shown in Salford's Chapel Street on a map published in 1794. The premises rapidly expanded in size and diversity until the old Iron Works was closed in 1938 and the business relocated to Newton Heath in Manchester.

The company's 'popular' neighbour Threlfalls's brewery eventually took over the works, complete with its legendary hole in the wall through which Mather & Platt workers had devised their own method of securing regular supplies of beer from their neighbours. One of Lowry's most famous works, painted in 1943, shows workers heading through the snow to Mather & Platt's factory gates.

VIMTO

With a £100 loan from his family, former stockbroker, clerk and soap factory manager John Noel Nichols started a small wholesale druggist and herbalist business in 1890. Eighteen years later he discovered the formulation for Vimto – a herbal tonic originally known as Vimtonic. The secret fruit and herb recipe has remained unchanged.

Promoted as a pick-me-up instilling 'vim and vigour', it was first produced in barrels and delivered at night to local temperance bars and cafés. Its popularity quickly spread and in 1910, J. N. Nichols & Co. became a registered business with premises in Chapel Street, Salford, which in 1806 became the first street in the country to be illuminated by gas.

Inside the Vimto works in 1928. (Courtesy of Nichols plc)

Vimto delivery vehicles, 1928. (Courtesy of Nichols plc)

Above: Inventor John Noel Nichols at the wheel of his car in 1922. (Courtesy of Nichols plc)

Left: Hiking girl advertisement in 1947. (Courtesy of Nichols plc)

Part of the Vimto Gardens development. (Courtesy of English Cities Fund)

Nine years later it was registered in Guyana and a year or so later a friend of Noel's, who worked as a representative in India for the Kiwi boot polish company, took samples of the concentrate to the subcontinent where it was bottled locally and became a favourite of British troops, reminding them of the 'taste of home'. It was the start of an export trade that established Vimto across the globe.

Vimto no longer has its headquarters in Salford but its name lives on in the shape of a multimillion-pound development of apartments, townhouses, shops and offices called Vimto Gardens, built only a stone's throw from the old Chapel Street premises.

CUSSONS

With its industrial heritage of mills, factories and foundries belching smoke over grimy Lowryesque back-to-back terraced houses, it is ironic that Salford is the home of one of the world's most luxurious soaps: Imperial Leather.

As long ago as 1768, Count Orlof, a Russian nobleman, commissioned a brand of perfume called Eau de Cologne Imperiale Russe from Bayleys of Bond Street in London. It was made using a high-quality Russian leather that produced a distinctive aroma from its birch oil tanning process. Some years later, in 1938, Alexander Tom Cussons, who had acquired Bayleys and was manufacturing soap from a factory built on farmland above an old bleach works in the Kersall Vale district of Salford, started to use the perfume, creating Imperial Leather and other toiletries. Originally it was called Imperial Russian Leather.

Alexander Tom Cussons was clearly a man with an appreciation of exotic aromas. At his home in Vine Street, Kersall, he had an impressive orchid collection and many of the flowers were featured in company advertisements for Imperial Leather with the tagline 'both

The Kersal Vale Works at Salford – now demolished. (Courtesy of PZ Cussons)

One of the old Cussons delivery vans. (Courtesy of PZ Cussons)

"JUST THE SOAP FOR YOUR BATH!"

Ivy soap

3d. PER LARGE DOUBLE CAKE.

IT FLOATS!

Is it not most annoying when having a bath to lose the soap or to find you have left it wasting in the water? Neither will happen with "IVY" Soap, which is always in sight, floating on the surface. Children are no longer any trouble on "Bath Night" when "IVY" Soap is used—they are so delighted to see it sailing on the water.

"IVY" Soap is a beautiful, white, "Milky" Soap, hard, and very lasting. Guaranteed pure and free from irritating chemicals. Gives a creamy lather, and is **SPLENDID FOR WASHING** Laces, Prints, Fine Underclothing, and all delicate goods, the colour and texture of which suffer damage from common soaps.

Ask your Grocer for "**IVY**" Soap. If any difficulty, we will send you 3 Cakes in a handy box, carriage paid, on receipt of your address and 12 Stamps, or 1s. Postal Order.

GOODWIN'S Ivy Soap Works, **SALFORD.**

Above left: One of the early advertisements for Imperial Leather with its orchid illustration. (Courtesy of PZ Cussons)

Above right: Goodwin's floating Ivy soap advertisement. (Courtesy of Grace's Guide to British Industrial History)

Left: A cake of Goodwin's Mother Shipton's 'witchcraft' soap. (Courtesy of the Museum of Witchcraft, Boscastle, Cornwall)

equally exquisite'. Regrettably, the whole collection was destroyed by a German bomb that landed at the bottom of his garden in 1941. It profoundly affected Alexander Cussons and he moved from Salford to south Manchester, where he felt he would be safe.

Just before the end of nineteenth century, people in and around Salford would have been familiar with one of the earliest motor cars, a Lutzmann-Benz being driven by another Salford soap manufacture, Charles Goodwin, with the life-sized figure of the folklore character Mother Shipton sitting in the passenger seat.

Born in Knaresborough, in the fifteenth century Mother Shipton was known as the nation's most remarkable prophetess – predicting, among other things, the Great Fire of London and the defeat of the Spanish Armada – and her witch-like image appears on one of the soaps made by G.W. Goodwin & Son at their Ivy Soap Works in Salford. A bar of the soap can be seen in the Witchcraft Museum on Cornwall.

Goodwin's also made what they called 'Just the soap for the bath' – a large double cake costing just 3d that appealed to children because it floated on the surface of the water. It was advertised as being ideal for 'laces, prints and fine underthings'. Goodwin's was taken over by Colgate Palmolive-Peet in 1938.

WARD & GOLDSTONE

In 1882, Meyer Hart Goldstone met James Henry Ward in a suburb of neighbouring Manchester forming the landmark Salford cable and accessories company of Ward & Goldstone with its headquarters in Frederick Road. It was to become one of the North West's biggest employers with factories on twelve different sites by 1975.

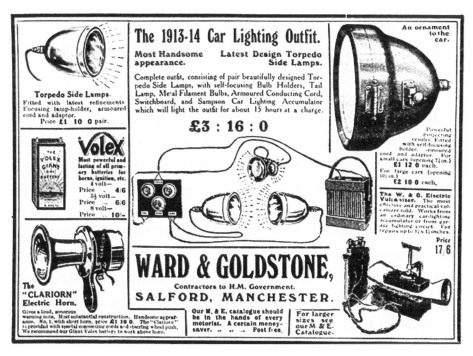

An advertisement for Ward & Goldstone's car lighting outfit costing £3 16s, 1913–14. (Courtesy of Grace's Guide to British Industrial History)

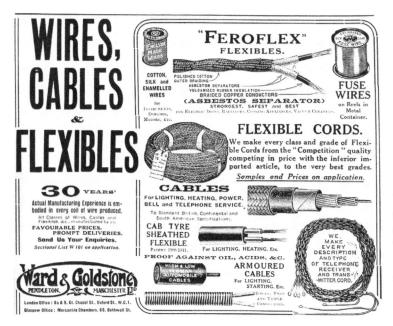

Wires, cables and flexibles advertised by Ward & Goldstone. (Courtesy of Grace's Guide to British Industrial History)

By 1900 it was sufficiently well established to be able to donate flexible cabling to the Transvaal war effort, and in 1910 they made the Atlantic wireless transmitter for the London department store, Gamages. During the 1980s, the company acquired a number of businesses run by Volex, the leading cable supplier, and shortly afterwards it became known as the Volex Group. The company was also one of the major suppliers of household electric goods to Woolworths. The Frederick Road factory was closed in 1986.

Today, the Ward & Goldstone legacy is perpetuated by Warrington-based Ionix Systems, manufacturers of high-performance wire systems for the aerospace and medical industries. They are part of the Amphenol Military Aerospace Operations division.

SEDDON CONSTRUCTION LTD

When brothers George and John Seddon from Little Hulton, Salford, started their business in 1897 they laid the foundations for a building empire that today is a nationwide company with a £200 million turnover and some 800 employees. It's all a far cry from the days when the two brothers travelled by horse and trap from one modest job to the next in and around their home.

Right from its early days as a growing business, Seddon has provided employment for large numbers of Salfordians, a practice that continues today with the fifth generation of the family at the helm.

Seddon secured the contracts to build all five housing estates in the founders' home town of Little Hulton, with many thousands of Salfordians moving into the area when the city embarked on its overspill policy, moving families from grim, substandard housing into homes where they had the luxury of inside baths and toilets.

Today, Seddon is one of the country's leading construction companies undertaking all types of building work including, hospitals, and health centres, schools, churches, hotels and leisure centres, retail and industrial premises as well as housing.

GREENGATE & IRWELL RUBBER CO.

Two Salford companies that manufactured waterproofs and rainwear both flourished in the North West's damp and rainy climate: the Greengate & Irwell Rubber Co. (off Ordsall Lane) and J. Mandleberg & Co.

Greengate & Irwell was formed as a public company in 1941 through the amalgamation of two other companies that had factories in Manchester, Radcliffe, London and Glasgow, one of which dated back to 1867 – the Isidor Frankenburg & Sons rubber-proofing business. At the Salford factory they produced rubber belting and tubing, hose, cables, proofed fabrics and waterproof clothing including rubber footwear.

Above: Still bearing the name – the Greengate and Irwell factory. The tower of Strangeways prison, Manchester, is in the background left. (Courtesy of photographer Aidan O'Rouke)

Right: Advertisement from 1890 for Mandleberg's waterproofs. (Courtesy of Grace's Guide to British Industrial History)

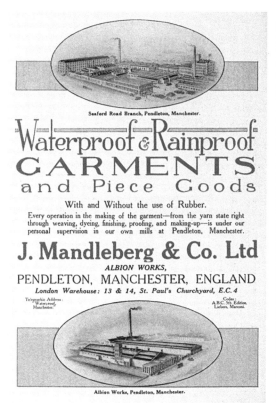

Above left: A 1920 Mandleberg advertisement showing their Albion Works at Pendleton. (Courtesy of Grace's Guide to British Industrial History)

Above right: A Valstar trench coat as worn by Humphrey Bogart in the film *Casablanca* in 1942. (Courtesy of Grace's Guide to British Industrial History)

The company prospered and by 1961 it had some 2,500 employees manufacturing an even wider range of goods that included rubber flooring, latex thread and a bigger range of outerwear and protective clothing. Some of the goods were made using the new 'plastic' rubber and balata, a hard-wearing rubber substitute made from the bully tree in South America. Greengate & Irwell was closed in the 1970s.

Originally India rubber manufacturers, J. Mandleberg & Co, occupied two huge factories in the Pendleton district – including the Albion Works dating back to the 1890s – where they fashioned a range of waterproof and rainproof garments sold through 'all leading drapers, mantle houses, ladies' and gentlemen's outfitters'. In 1937, just a few years before the outbreak of the Second World War, they began to manufacture fabrics that were also gasproof and the Valstar flying suit.

A decade later, in 1947, they exhibited sixteen trademarked products at the British industries fair, including weather and travel wear, gabardines, linings, hospital sheets and even hot-water bottles. In the same year they changed their name to Valstar & J. Mandleberg Co., having merged with the Italian-based company of that name.

Established in 1911, Valstar today continues to allude to its association with Mandleberg as the British company 'aiming at producing the best raincoats in the world for the stylish man'.

Audrey Hepburn and Humphrey Bogart, with his iconic trench coat in *Casablanca*, were just two of the cinema stars who sported Valstar rainwear. The company has its headquarters in Verrone and its showrooms in Milan.

GEC

'Everything electrical', that's how the giant GEC (General Electric Company) described itself, and it all began in Salford. Originally established as the General Electrical Apparatus Co., it changed its name to GEC in 1886 and produced its first catalogue a year later. One year after that – 1888 – it opened its first factory. This was known as the Manchester Works even though it was in Salford, and a second factory, the Peel Works, was opened overlooking Salford's Peel Park.

From modest beginnings – manufacturing telephones, electric bells, ceiling roses and switches, lamps, lightbulbs, batteries and electrical accessories – it was to spread its wings across the country, becoming a major UK-based industrial conglomerate with interests in defence, electronics, engineering and consumer products.

During the First World War, GEC contributed to the war effort by making a vast range of products including radios, signalling lamps, arc lamp carbons as well as power plants for munitions works and ships.

An early GEC advertisement by Salford Electrical Instruments Ltd. (Courtesy of Grace's Guide to British Industrial History)

B·O·A·C COMET 4

G.E.C. equipped galley

NO LESS THAN 77 OF THE WORLD'S AIRLINES USE *G.E.C.* AIRBORNE GALLEY EQUIPMENT

No-one else, anywhere in the world, supplies anything like as much aircraft catering equipment as does the G.E.C., indisputably the foremost company in this specialised field.

THE GENERAL ELECTRIC COMPANY LIMITED, MAGNET HOUSE, KINGSWAY, LONDON, W.C.2.

Above: A GEC advertisement noting that seventy-seven of the world's airlines use their galley equipment. (Courtesy of Grace's Guide to British Industrial History)

Left: Wartime advertisement by GEC in 1944. (Courtesy of Grace's Guide to British Industrial History)

NO DOUBT WHICH IS THE BETTER WEAPON

—no doubt, either, which is the more necessary —to hasten the day when we can go forward to better times, new standards of living. When that day comes there will be better G.E.C. Electric Appliances to give you a fresh conception of the benefits and convenience of electricity in the home.

G.E.C.

HOUSEHOLD ELECTRIC APPLIANCES

Advt. of The General Electric Co., Ltd., Magnet House, Kingsway, W.C.2

After the war it seamlessly made the switch from wartime production to peacetime activities, developing a programme capable of meeting any electrical contract. In 1919, it absorbed the whole of the Osram light bulb company. Similarly, during the Second World War, when the company had some 40,000 employers around the UK, GEC was a major supplier to the military of electrical and engineering products, several representing significant technological advances.

In 1936, a GEC television set was first demonstrated at Wembley receiving signals from the BBC transmitter at Alexandra Park and in 1956 it began to manufacture TV sets for consumers.

There then followed a number of significant takeovers, mergers and acquisitions as well as the formation of numerous subsidiary companies. GEC, as a company under that name, became defunct in 1999.

CO-OPERATIVE WHOLESALE SOCIETY

The Co-operative movement – or the Co-op as it has always been affectionately known – has its origins and roots firmly embedded in the North West of England. In Salford it played a key role in ensuring that during some of the hardest times in the city's history – and elsewhere in the country, too – that there was, at least, always a good brew to put the world to rights.

In December 1930, more than 1,000 VIPs and specially invited guests gathered in Ordsall Lane in Salford to witness the opening of a 'handsome' new tea-packing factory and warehouse alongside the Manchester Ship Canal. Earlier, on the same day as the official opening, the SS *Makalla* had sailed into Salford Docks with an 'unprecedented direct cargo' of 8 million pounds in weight of tea from India to be stored in the new English and Scottish CWS warehouse.

Everyone who attended the official opening received a souvenir pamphlet and a decorated tin bearing a photograph of the giant new warehouse on the lid and containing samples of the Co-op tea. The popularity of the opening, in fact, was such that it was extended into the following day so many hundreds more people could visit the site and look around the building.

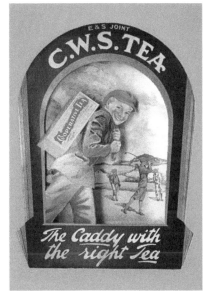

'The Caddy with the right Tea' – a CWS advertisement. (Courtesy of Historyworld, brian@wiganworld.co.uk)

Above left: Clothing sold by CWS. (Courtesy of Grace's Guide to British Industrial History)

Above right: The CWS proudly enters the new Elizabethan era. (Courtesy of Grace's Guide to British Industrial History)

The land on which the warehouse stood was owned by the Manchester Ship Canal Co., making it a prime location for ocean steamers and liners to unload their cargoes of tea straight into the warehouse. In fact, one of the steamships operated by the CWS, *The Pioneer*, was the first commercial vessel to use the Ship Canal.

Salford was also home to the CWS Broughton Cabinet Works that occupied two adjoining factories in Trafalgar Street, the first purchased in 1891 and the second in 1900. Together with another large factory, the Pelaw Cabinet Works in Gateshead, the Broughton Works manufactured what was described in the society's official history as 'honest furniture free from the innumerable deceptions of the "garret masters" and the cheap and showy shops'. The second of the two Broughton factories was also used for tailoring, an industry practised by the CWS in Salford since 1895.

BETFRED

Carpets, coffee and civility, that was the 'secret' formula that elevated the young twenty-four-year-old Fred Done from the back streets of Salford to become a billionaire and the most successful independent bookmaker in the world. It is a true rags-to-riches story.

Fred Done's first betting shop in Salford. (Courtesy of Betfred)

Fred Done in his Warrington headquarters office with a framed old map of Salford behind him. (Courtesy of Betfred)

With just £75, Fred and his brother Peter opened their first betting shop in the legendary Salford area of Whit Lane in Pendleton in 1967. At the time, shortly after the end of illegal back-alley bookies, betting shops were dreary, austere and unwelcoming places. Fred recognised that they were desperately in need of an image makeover. He carpeted the floor, laid on free coffee for his customers and insisted that the men were also called 'sir'. It was a masterstroke that changed the image of the hole-in-the-wall betting shop forever.

The business took off from day one, and over the next ten years he had opened further thirty shops with more coming on stream year by year. One of the shops he bought was owned by Salford's other famous bookmaker, 'Honest' Albert Finney, father of the much-acclaimed actor Albert Finney. Today, Fred (who at seventy-four is still at the helm of the international BetFred empire) has 1,700 shops, employs more than 11,000 people – 450 of

From small beginnings ... a modern operations room. (Courtesy of Betfred)

them at the company's Warrington headquarters – and has an annual turnover of more than £8 billion and growing.

Fred, who still lives in his native Salford (but in somewhat grander style than the terrace in former Hyde Street in Ordsall where he was born), confesses that he was a poor scholar who hated school but who always had an innate talent for making money – a fact reinforced each year when he appears on the *Sunday Times* 'Rich List'. Apart from BetFred, he owns Chelmsford Racecourse and the company sponsors the rugby Super League and the World Snooker Championships. He also has an interest in a number of major companies including two insurance companies, construction and development companies, health and safety businesses, a sports tour business, two park-and-feed truck stops, a mobile app development company and also an online business. His brother Peter runs the successful Peninsula Service business centre across the border in central Manchester.

SALFORD VAN HIRE

'Big oaks from little acorns grow' is a saying that could have been inspired by the story of Salford Van Hire. The company was formed in 1965 by Raffaello Bacci, who left his native Tuscany in Italy in the 1950s aged just thirteen to live with his grandfather, Felice Bacci, in Salford. After leaving St Boniface's School he started work in his grandfather's business making ornamental statuettes and lampshades and it was there where the spark of his entrepreneurial flair was ignited.

He quickly realised that he could earn a few extra pounds by renting out his van when it was not required for deliveries in and around area. Such was the demand he soon had to

Company founder Raffaello Bacci with two vehicles from the 6,000-strong fleet. (Courtesy of Salford Van Hire)

Three sizes of vehicle outside Manchester United's ground. (Courtesy of Salford Van Hire)

buy another van and then a third, laying the foundations of what was to become one of the country's biggest car and commercial vehicle-hire companies, with a current annual turnover in excess of £45 million.

After just five years at its original premises in Salford's Camp Street, just a stone's throw from Raffaello's school, the company had to relocate to larger premises in Sherbourne Street, Manchester (now its UK headquarters) and sometime later to a second depot in Leeds. The company now operates a fleet of more than 6,000 light, media and heavy vehicles for both long and short rental. Four decades after its formation, Raffaello still remains at the helm as chairman, now helped by other close members of the Bacci family.

PILKINGTON'S TILE & POTTERY COMPANY

It was as result of a fortuitous coincidence, coupled with opportunism and technical know-how, that the much-acclaimed Pilkington's Tile & Pottery Company was established in 1892 in a factory in Clifton, Salford, alongside the now derelict Fletcher's Canal.

Above: The former Pilkington's Tile & Pottery factory at Clifton Junction, Salford. (Courtesy of Salford Local History Library Collection)

Below: Artist and designer William Slater Mycock at his workbench at Pilkington's. (Courtesy of Salford Local History Library Collection)

A lustre ware vase painted by
William Slater Mycock.
(Courtesy of AD Antiques,
www.adantiques.com)

Some three years earlier the Clifton & Kearsley Coal Co. sank a pair of pit shafts to tap into the coal seams lying adjacent to the 20-mile-long Pendleton Fault through the Irwell Valley. Unfortunately, due to excessive amounts of water flooding the shafts, the work became increasingly hazardous and the quest for coal was abandoned. However, believing they could turn adversity to advantage, the four Pilkington brothers decided to use the excavated lime-rich clay and salt marl to make glazed bricks, but it was found to be unsuitable.

The ultimate answer came as a result of a happy coincidence. By chance, the coal company knew William Barton, a chemist who worked for Josiah Wedgwood & Sons, who analysed the marl, concluding that it could be used to make decorative tiles that were highly fashionable at the time. By 1903, the factory diversified, developing an opalescent ceramic glaze that, along with glazes that followed, was used to manufacture exquisite lustre ware vases and bowls that were sold by some of the top retailers, including Liberty & Co. After a visit from George V in 1913, the factory was awarded the royal warrant. At the end of the 1930s, the production of the art pottery ceased but the manufacture of tiles continued. Pilkington's Royal Lancastrian lustre ware is now much sought after by collectors and pieces can sell for four- and five-figure sums. Several examples of Pilkington's pottery and tiles can now be seen in a dedicated permanent exhibition at Salford Museum.

BREWING

Salford has a long and proud brewing tradition that is perpetuated today by the production of craft beers by local artisan breweries. Until relatively recent times, the pub was the only affordable leisure refuge for the mill and factory workers of Salford – before the slum clearances of the 1960s and 1970s, there was a local on virtually every street corner. In the old Cross Lane area, bordering the former dockland, there were reputedly more pubs per square mile than almost anywhere else in Britain, and in many of the less salubrious ones the tables were chained to the floor to prevent them being hurled across the taproom in drunken brawls.

The old Cobden Hotel in the Brindle Heath area of Salford. (Author's collection)

One of the scores of Salford pubs demolished in the slum clearance programme. (Author's collection)

It was this thirst for beer that from Victorian times until the renaissance of the 'new' Salford gave rise to the establishment of brewery giants such as Groves and Whitnall, which was formed in 1868 when the family patriarch, William Peer Grimble Groves (who had vinegar works in Manchester) bought the Bathe & Newbolds Brewery in Regent Road, Salford. By 1888, when the firm incorporated and became Groves & Whitnall Ltd, the factory had been completely rebuilt, employing hundreds of local people.

One of the original partners, Arthur William Whitnall, who died at the early age of forty-two, played a key role in the brewery's success by securing as their head brewer the services of Charles Henry Hill, who worked for a small rival firm in Manchester and who had a reputation for producing an exceptionally good brew. Before offering him the job, Whitnall systematically sampled all the various beers that were available at the time in Salford and Manchester, settling eventually on the one produced by Mr Hill at a small brewery in Ardwick, Manchester.

In a newspaper advertisement in 1940, the brewery declared 'The Gateway to Salford begins at Groves and Whitnall', and listed what it described as its 'halting places' in the city: 'The Bridge Inn (music), The Regatta Inn, The Grove Inn, The Gas Tavern, The Fox Vaults (famous all over the world), the Borough Inn, The Star Inn (music).' All had their popular Amber Ale on tap, which the advertisement proclaimed as 'something quite different … There is nothing quite like it'.

In 1903, the Groves family were responsible for founding the legendary Salford Lads' Club, which was officially opened on 30 January 1904 by Robert Baden-Powell, founder of the Scout movement. In a survey by the *Manchester Evening News*, the Ordsall Club (featured on the cover of The Smiths' *The Queen is Dead* album) was voted the third most iconic building in the UK.

Left: Threlfall's Cork Street brewery, now the Deva City Office Park. (Courtesy of the Deva City Office Park)

Below: Now smart new offices, the former Threlfall's brewery. (Courtesy of the Deva City Office Park)

The seven brothers of Seven Bro7hers Brewery. *Left to right*: Luke, Dan, Guy, Nathan, Greg, Kit and Keith. (Courtesy of Seven Bro7thers Brewery)

Another of Salford's brewing giants was Threlfall's. In 1895, the Threlfall Brewery Co. bought the Blue Lion public house in Salford's Cook Street and developed the site as the multistorey Cook Street Brewery, continuing to supply scores of public houses and hotels throughout the North West until 1967. In 1988, the brewery, with its landmark tower, was given a Grade II listing, but it fell into increasing dereliction until 2000 when it was taken over by the Deva Project and developed sympathetically as a modern business centre with self-contained office suites arranged around a central courtyard. Many of the building's original architectural features, including the tower, have been retained.

For beer drinkers in Salford today, as well as in other parts of the country, there is now a new kid on the block: the appropriately named Seven Bro7hers Brewery, which produces a range of bottled, keg and canned craft beers from its premises in Salford Quays. The seven brothers in question, who all have roles in the burgeoning business, are Guy, Keith, Luke, Dan, Nathan, Kit and Greg, the sons of the Salford-born keen home-brewing enthusiast Eric McAvoy and his wife Freda.

It was all very much a home-spun affair, until Kit travelled to Oslo in Norway where he became aware and inspired by the growing interest in craft beers. On his return to Salford he transmitted his enthusiasm to his brothers and in 2014 they launched their own brewery, quickly moving to new and bigger premises. Their range of ales is now distributed to pubs and bars throughout Salford and Manchester as well as other parts of the UK, and an export trade is on the horizon. Inspired by their brothers' success, their four sisters have started their own gin-making business.

The working men's pub, with its no-frills vault and taproom, can still be seen in the 'old' Salford captured on canvas by Lowry, but they are fast disappearing in the wake of trendy restaurant bars and eateries where the traditional pint now competes with a glass of wine or a cocktail.

JEWISH IMMIGRANTS

A significant proportion of businesses in Salford, including many that became major employers, were established by Jewish immigrant families, often fleeing persecution in Europe. They brought with them the traditional trades and skills practised in their homelands, many of which, and especially those involving the various facets of the cotton and textile industries, found a ready market and prospered in Salford.

The influx began in the mid-nineteenth century with a steady trickle of Jews arriving in Manchester where there was an established Jewish population dating back to 1780, but also increasingly to bordering districts of Salford such as Broughton.

Among the first to arrive were merchants from central Europe (many of them political refugees) and later Jewish families from Romania fleeing the persecution of 1869, as well as young men who were in danger of being forced to serve in the Russian army. The greatest number, however, came in the wake of the prolonged Russo-Polish migrations, which lasted for more than thirty years – from 1881 to 1914.

Many of the earliest immigrants became waterproof garment manufacturers, an industry developed in their native lands that they could easily adapt to the rainy climate of Salford

Sid Sidney Hamburger. (Courtesy of Searchlight Electric)

Searchlight Electric's modern showroom. (Courtesy of Searchlight Electric)

and North West England. Others, especially the Russo-Polish immigrants, were able to find business openings for cap making and tailoring skills, while still others became jewellery 'knockers' (buying and selling jewellery door-to-door), street traders and hawkers.

One of the greatest success stories is that of Searchlight Electric. It was started in 1954 by the late Sidney Hamburger in a cellar at No. 1b Cooper Street, Salford, which today is a global supplier of decorative lighting with a joint-venture factory in China. Born in Salford in 1914, Sidney Hamburger was the son of Polish immigrant parents who fled their native country to escape the pogroms of the late 1890s.

After leaving Salford Grammar School he started his working life selling kettles, irons, heaters and decorative Christmas lights, travelling around the country with samples. In 1949, just four years after establishing his business, he moved to larger premises in Blackfriars Street, followed by further moves to Middlewood Street in 1960 and Water Street in 1980 as the business expanded.

His reputation as a respected and successful businessman resulted in him receiving a CBE in 1966 and a knighthood in 1981. He was also a former mayor of Salford and in 1971 was appointed chairman of the former North Western Regional Health Authority. Sir Sidney died at the age of eighty-six in 2001, just a short time before the Earl and Countess of Wessex opened Searchlight Electric's new showroom and warehouse on an 8.5-acre site at Newton Heath, Manchester. The family-run business is now headed by Managing Director Daniel Hamburger, the third generation of the family.

Salford also played a pivotal role in the success of another knight of the realm, Sir Montague Burton, who started his working life as a hawker pedalling his wares in and around Broughton and neighbouring Cheetham Hill in Manchester, and who went on to found the world's biggest and best-known bespoke tailoring empire.

Left: Sir Montague Burton (left) on a visit to one of his factories. (Courtesy of Burton Menswear, London)

Below: Machinists at work in the former Burton factory in Salford. (Courtesy of Burton Menswear, London)

Born Meshe David Osinsky in 1885 in Kaunas (in what is now Lithuania), he fled to Britain in 1900 to escape the Russian pogroms, settling in Cheetham Hill a year later where he found himself in an area populated by scores of other Jewish immigrant families who had come to Britain under similar circumstances. His business as a street vendor clearly prospered because, some two years later, he was able to establish a general outfitters in Chesterfield selling ready-made suits bought from a wholesaler. It was a fledgling business that would develop into one of the largest chains of clothing shops with a presence in almost every major town and city across the country until the late twentieth century: the Burton Menswear and Burton of London brands.

One of the company's iconic art deco clothing factories, the Burtonville Clothing Works, which became a landmark alongside the East Lancashire Road at Worsley in Salford, was opened by the Earl of Derby in 1938. At the peak of its production it employed some 4,000 workers. It closed in the 1970s and the building was demolished.

By 1913 Montague Maurice Burton had five men's tailoring shops, headquarters in Sheffield and manufacturing in Leeds. By 1939 the number had rocketed to some 400, including numerous factories like the one in Salford. During the Second World War, Burton made a quarter of the British military uniforms and around a third of all demob suits. He was knighted in 1931 for 'services to industrial relations' and in 1944 he was made an honorary doctorate at the University of Leeds. He died at the age of sixty-seven in 1952 while making an after-dinner speech in Leeds. He and his wife, Sophie Amelia Marks, had three sons and one daughter.

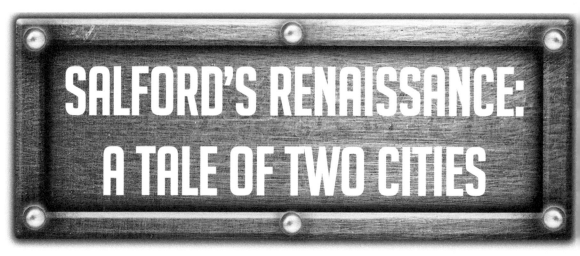

SALFORD'S RENAISSANCE: A TALE OF TWO CITIES

S alford's story since the advent of the Industrial Revolution is a tale of two cities – a story of rise and fall, and rise again.

Since the early years of the noughties, its fortunes as a place of business and industry have been riding high. The city is now recognised as one of the economic powerhouses of the North West, increasingly attracting new businesses and investors with the redeveloped Salford Quays (the former docks) – the prime location.

Such has been the growth in recent years, Salford is now ranked as the UK's number-one city for business start-ups, outstripping London and its neighbour Manchester. Overall, Salford has

A 'dank and dismal' wartime landscape – the Adelphi district alongside the River Irwell painted by L. S. Lowry in 1944. (Courtesy of The Lowry Centre)

An aerial view of Salford Docks, 1963. (Courtesy of Peel Group Archives)

approaching 9,000 businesses, employing around 130,000 people – a high proportion of them in digital, high-tech industries incubated and developed by Salford University.

Yet as recently as thirty or forty years ago, certainly well within living memory for many of its population, Salford was in the doldrums, beset by a wave after wave of setbacks that saw the city fall into a steady decline. By 1939, the once flourishing coal-mining industry at Worsley and Agecroft had all but ground to a halt. By the late 1960s or early 1970s, Salford's cotton mills – like those throughout Lancashire – were closing at a rate of one every week in the wake of foreign competition and the rising price of raw cotton.

The biggest blow of all, however, came in 1982 when the last ships loaded and unloaded their cargoes and Salford Docks was closed. The Ship Canal, which linked the docks to the world's ocean trade routes, was not deep enough for the massive new container vessels and, coupled with an increase in trade with Europe and the Far East, trade through Salford Docks dramatically decreased over a number of years until it could continue no more.

The docks, which during the early part of the nineteenth century had been the hub of the waterway artery that had pumped new blood into the heart of Salford's industrial revolution, was virtually overnight a lifeless, derelict wasteland with the loss of more than 3,000 jobs.

Whether it has been a case of boom or slump, the Ship Canal and the docks have been the predominant catalyst that has played a key role in the ebb and flow of Salford's industrial and economic fortunes. Together, they provided the impetus that fuelled Salford's textile mills and burgeoning engineering companies during the time when they were world leaders, and from the mid-1980s they have literally provided the foundations for the regeneration of the Salford of the twenty-first century. It has been an unparalleled tale of two cities.

SALFORD QUAYS

The regeneration began in 1983–84 when Salford City Council acquired a 220-acre section of the docks from the Manchester Ship Canal Co. and two years later developers Urban Waterside started work on the multimillion-pound Salford Quays Development Plan. It was a massive undertaking, which echoed the same pioneering spirit of the navvies who dug out the first sods of earth to build the Ship Canal almost a hundred years earlier.

It was, above all, a visionary plan for the future that, as a complete contrast to the vestiges of the old Salford on its doorstep, would embrace the performing and visual arts, a museum, an all-weather indoor shopping mall, an eclectic mix of modern houses and flats as well as sports and leisure facilities. The residential waterside developments echo the maritime history with names that include Merchants Quay, Grain Wharf and Labrador Quay.

Construction work begins in 2007. (Courtesy of Peel Group Archives)

Above: Cranes pierce the skyline as work on the new Salford gets under way. (Jefferson Air Photography)

Below: Salford Quays at night. (Courtesy of Peel Group Archives)

Above: A city for the twenty-first century – a panorama of Salford Quays. (Courtesy of Peel Group Archives)

Below: The Lowry Centre at Salford Quays. (Courtesy of The Lowry Centre)

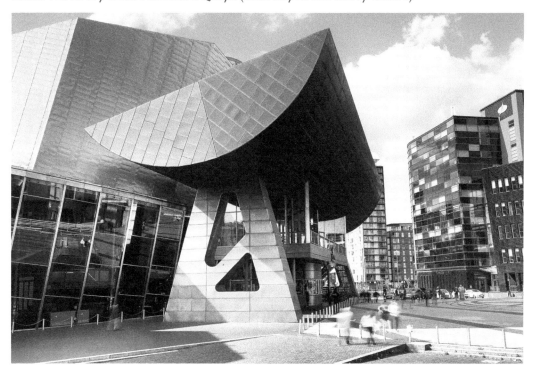

THE LOWRY

Salford's Victorian music hall-style theatres – The Hippodrome and The Windsor – had long since played to their last audiences and fallen victim to demolition, so early in the planning stage of the Quays the need for a new landmark theatre became a priority.

Above: The Lowry
Gallery, housing
the largest single
collection of the
artist's work.
(Courtesy of The
Lowry Centre)

Right: Typical Salford
street scene – *Man
of Wall* by L. S. Lowry.
His initials are on the
suitcase. (Courtesy
of The Lowry
Centre)

The project was launched in 1994 and some six years later on 20 April 2000, The Lowry Theatre was opened at the end of Pier 8, quickly becoming an all-year entertainment venue offering a diverse programme of theatre, opera, musicals, dance, music and comedy for young and old alike from Salford and far beyond.

With its backing from Salford City Council and Arts Council England, The Lowry passionately pursues a policy of nurturing new talent 'developing creative professionals of the future and raising aspirations'. Additionally, it has an active community work programme across the city and a youth employment scheme that engages with young people aged fourteen to

A northern market scene by L. S. Lowry, probably Salford. (Courtesy of The Lowry Centre)

twenty-four from Salford and beyond who are being assisted by NEET (the Not in Education, Employment or Training scheme).

The landmark centre's gallery is also home to the largest collection of works of artist L. S. Lowry, the most evocative of which, with their 'matchstick men and dogs', depict Salford's old cotton mills and the terraced streets where their workers lived. Within The Lowry, too, is the appropriately named Pier Eight, a stylish restaurant and bar with tables overlooking the waterside.

IMPERIAL WAR MUSEUM NORTH

Salford Docks and the surrounding Trafford Park area – where factories manufactured munitions, tanks and machines to support the war effort – were a major target for German bombers during the Blitz in December 1940. In all, some 200 people, including dock workers, were killed in and around the dockland area. The area on which the Imperial War Museum North now stands was the site of the gigantic Hovis grain silos that were built in 1906. They were destroyed by enemy aircraft in the 1940 air raid and rebuilt in 1953. Shrapnel and an anti-aircraft shell were found during the digging of the foundations for the war museum, which was opened in 2000.

Designed by the Polish-American architect Daniel Libeskind, whose parents survived the Holocaust, the museum's strangely angled walls and ceilings are a metaphor for a war-shattered world as well as a memorial to the men and women who were killed by the

Above: The Imperial War Museum North at Salford Quays. (Courtesy of Bitter Bredt)

Right: Architect Daniel Libeskind. (Courtesy of Stefan Ruiz)

German bombs. Libeskind was the architect who won the 2002 competition for the master plan for the reconstruction of the World Trade Centre in New York. He also designed the Jewish Museum in Berlin.

TALK TALK

One of the Salford's iconic industrial landmarks, the Soapworks factory on Ordsall Lane, formerly occupied by Colgate-Palmolive, has been transformed from an industrial shell into the northern headquarters of the telecommunications company Talk Talk. Its 106,000 square

Above: One of Salford's best-known landmarks, the Soapworks – now northern headquarters for Talk Talk. (Courtesy of Talk Talk)

Below: The roof terrace with views across the Quays. (Courtesy of Talk Talk)

feet has been designed to provide ultra-modern office space for the 1,500 personnel while at the same time incorporating features that showcase the building's heritage. This includes the use of more than 500 bars of soap to create a quirky and aromatic fireplace art installation.

After searching the region for suitable new headquarters, Talk Talk moved to the Soapworks from their previous offices at Warrington so that they could be close to the plethora of digital and high-tech communications businesses in MediaCityUK.

The new headquarters includes a 350-seat restaurant and café that leads out onto a rooftop garden and a dedicated picnic area for relaxation and informal meetings, complete with artificial grass, deck chairs and picnic blankets for chilly days. There is also a rooftop herb garden that provides many of the ingredients for dishes such as chilli, lasagne and salads served in the restaurant. Talk Talk moved into the Soapworks in June 2017.

COPTHORNE HOTEL

In the very early stages of the development of Salford Quays, a decision was taken to build a hotel that would be able to cater for the anticipated influx of people visiting the area from other parts of the country and also from overseas. The four-star Copthorne Hotel, which is part of the Millennium Hotel Group, was opened in 1985, providing 166 en suite rooms, meeting room facilities and a canalside restaurant, the Clipper Brasserie, offering British and international cuisine. The hotel now has some seventy staff.

Salford's quayside Copthorne Hotel. (Courtesy of Millennium Hotels)

MEDIACITYUK

Rising above the former wasteland of the docks, MediaCityUK is now firmly established as the home of the BBC, ITV, dock10 studios, the University of Salford and some 250 creative, digital and technology companies – and by around 2030 it is expected to double in size.

MediaCity, 2016. (Courtesy of Peel Group Archives)

Above: Workers relax in a green 'oasis' at MediaCity. (Courtesy of Peel Group Archives)

Below: Reflections on the past – MediaCity glistens on the former dockland waterway. (Courtesy of Peel Group Archives)

This once barren piece of brownfield land that served as a car park for The Lowry is now a vibrant community of 7,000 people, ironically significantly more than the entire cloth-capped, 5,000-strong army of dockers who laboured in the port in its heyday.

Building work on MediaCityUK started in June 2007 as a joint venture between the Peel Group and General Capital, who together now have ambitious plans to double its size with £1 billion of private investment. The Peel Group – who own the Manchester Ship Canal and the Bridgewater Canal – is today one of the UK's leading infrastructure, transport and real estate investors with a business portfolio of more than £5 billion.

Between 1971 and 1987, the family of company founder John Whittaker acquired the iconic Lancashire-based textile businesses of Peel Mills and John Bright & Brother as well as the Bridgewater estates and the Manchester Ship Canal, laying the foundations on which the business now stands.

BBC NORTH

In April 2011 the BBC relocated a number of its key departments to a new state-of-the-art creative hub at MediaCity. Today there are more than 3,000 full-time staff working in 26 departments including BBC Children's, BBC Learning, BBC Radio 5 live, BBC Sport, BBC Radio Manchester and BBC Breakfast as well as Religion and Ethics, the BBC Philharmonic and parts of Research and Development, Drama and Comedy.

Many of the BBC's most popular programme are made in MediaCityUK, among them *Match of the Day, Blue Peter, Mastermind, Dragon's Den, Songs of Praise* and *You and Yours*. All in all, more than 35,000 hours of BBC radio and TV content are produced at BBC North in Salford

Smart and functional – the interior of BBC North, MediaCity. (Courtesy of BBC North)

The distinctive relaxation and interview pods at BBC North. (Courtesy of BBC North)

each year. In much the same way as two centuries ago – when Salford's engineering pioneers were inventing machines to change the industrial world at the time – technical experts now working for BBC Digital at Salford are discovering new and exciting ways of advancing the horizons of the world of mass media.

Their ultimate aim at Salford Quays is to work exclusively with tapeless, file-based technology that will help to make BBC North 'the most advanced broadcasting centre in Europe'. Tapeless technology developed in Salford has already enabled programme makers to deliver twenty-four channels of sporting coverage at any one time.

The move to MediaCityUK also had one unexpected benefit. For Salfordians it ended a long-standing irritant that went back to the early days of broadcasting. Until the BBC established its new northern home in Salford, the corporation's London-based broadcasters invariably pronounced the name of the city as 'Sal-ford' as in Sally and not 'Sol-ford' as is correct, much to the amusement – and slight annoyance – of the locals. Now it is rarely, if ever, mispronounced.

ITV

With the arrival of ITV in 2013 and the move of *Coronation Street* a year later from Manchester's city centre back to its Salford roots, MediaCityUK became Europe's largest TV, radio and media communications hub. It completed ITV's move out of Manchester and into its new flagship, five-storey Orange Tower headquarters close to the BBC and some of the country's most exciting digital and high-tech companies.

Collectively, ITV now has around 950 staff based in the various tower departments and *Coronation Street* and, with the addition of new production support buildings now in the pipeline, numbers are expected to increase.

Apart from 'Corrie', several other popular programmes are produced from Salford, among them are *The Jeremy Kyle Show*, *Judge Rinder*, *Countdown*, *University Challenge* and several recordings of *The Voice*. The daily news programmes from *Granada Reports* are also broadcast from the Orange Tower.

Above: ITV's building at MediaCity. (Courtesy of ITV Studios)

Left: Granada TV's former studios – the 'birthplace' of *Coronation Street*. (Courtesy of ITV Studios)

In producing *Coronation Street* from studios at the Quays, the long-running soap has, in fact, returned to its spiritual home, just walking distance from Archie Street – the small terraced street in the Ordsall district that provided the drama's creator, Salford-born TV screenwriter the late Tony Warren, with the conceptual inspiration. The first episode was screened in 1960, and from 1964 to 1969 Archie Street was featured in the programme's title sequence with a cat centre-stage on one of the walls of the back-to-back houses. In 1936, No. 9 Archie Street was the real-life birthplace of Manchester United's 'Busby Babe' Eddie Colman, who died in the Munich air disaster of 1958 along with twenty-two others, among them six other team-mates.

Tony Warren's original vision was of a gutsy kitchen sink serial that eavesdropped on the day-to-day lives of working-class people. In that sense, during the first decade or so it mirrored for many Salfordians their own existence in what was once one of the most deprived slum areas of the country. The first twelve episodes were written by Tony Warren himself. He was also responsible for all the original characters, among them Ken Barlow, Ena Sharples, Elsie Tanner and Annie Walker.

The late Tony Warren, creator of *Coronation Street*. (Courtesy of ITV Studios)

Salford legend Violet Carson as battleaxe Ena Sharples in *Coronation Street*. (Courtesy of ITV Studios)

DOCK10

In the original grand plan for Salford Docks, provision was made for a No. 10 Dock, but it was never completed. The proposed site, however, has appropriately now been developed to provide ten state-of-the-art production studios for both the BBC and ITV.

The quayside dock10 development – which can be accessed by small vessels – provides employment for 150 people and is recognised as one of Europe's leading dedicated studios offering access to HD TV, digital post-production, cloud media management and advanced connectivity options across all digital platforms.

In March 2012, the Queen, accompanied by the Duke of Edinburgh, visited dock10 to perform the official opening of the studios. The royal couple watched rehearsals for *Football Focus* then visited the studios used for children's TV, including *Blue Peter* and *Newsround*. In dock10's Philharmonic Studio, the Queen enjoyed a performance by the BBC Philharmonic and the Salford Family Orchestra before unveiling a commemorative plaque.

The dock10 studios are also strategically sited alongside the University of Salford, facilitating the teaching of TV programming and production to the next generation with talented students coming from the length and breadth of the country.

March 2012: The Queen arrives at the dock10 studios for the official opening of MediaCity. (Courtesy of dock10)

Flag-waving schoolchildren outside dock10 at the opening of MediaCityUK by the Queen in March 2012. (Courtesy of dock10)

A still from Red Production's *Last Tango in Halifax*. (Courtesy of Red Production Company)

RED PRODUCTION COMPANY

MediaCityUK is also home of Red Production Co., an independent and innovative TV production company that has produced some of the country's most popular and critically acclaimed drama series including *Queer as Folk* by Russel T. Davies, *Happy Valley*, *Last Tango in Halifax*, *Ordinary Lies*, *Trust Me* and Paul's Abbott's *Clocking Off*.

The company was founded in 1998 by former script editor Nicola Shindler with fellow Mancunian Andrew Critchley. She is now executive producer and Andrew is managing director. The company employs twenty-eight full-time members of staff as well as hundreds of freelance crew while filming over the course of a year. It is also especially proud of its reputation and track record for providing a creative platform for new writing talent. It moved to MediaCityUK in 2012, having previously operated from an office at the former Granada studios in Manchester. In 2013, Red became part of the global company StudioCanal.

BUPA

International health insurance and healthcare provider Bupa has chosen Salford's MediaCity as the home for 2,400 of its Manchester-based support employees – the majority of its customer service centre personnel in the UK. This includes the specialist, dedicated support personnel for oncology and cardiac care, obstetrics and gynaecology, mental health and musculoskeletal disorders. The oncology service also offers a 'survivorship programme' and support for patients who have a terminal cancer diagnosis.

Now seventy years old, Bupa has more than 16 million health insurance customers, provides healthcare for more than 10 million people worldwide and employs 80,000 people across the UK and ten other markets globally.

BARCLAYS EAGLE LAB

Opened in November 2016, the Barclays Bank organisation chose The Landing at MediaCityUK as the venue for its first innovative business support learning and activity Eagle Lab in the North of England 'drawing on the city's vibrant start-up culture and rich industrial past'.

Inset: Creating for the future – young innovators at work in the Eagle Lab. (Courtesy of Barclays)
Above: Barclay's Eagle Lab at MediaCityUK. (Courtesy of Barclays)

The Salford Lab is one of thirteen across the UK offering office space for entrepreneurs and start-up businesses round-the-clock, seven-day-a-week access to a range of support services including mentoring. In tandem with the surrounding high-tech environment of MediaCityUK, it offers a wide range of specialist services and facilities including rapid product prototyping (techniques for fabricating scale models using 3D computer-aided technology), the use of 3D printers and collaborative, intense brainstorming 'hackathons' aimed at creating exciting new computer software.

ENER-G

With a workforce of more than 250 employees, the combined heat and power (CHP) energy supplier ENER-G Cogen International was founded in 1984 with headquarters in Daniel Adamson Road on the fringes of MediaCityUK. The company was acquired by Centrica plc in 2016 for £146 million.

The focus of the Salford operation is based on the design, installation and maintenance of gas-fuelled combined heat and power systems for industrial and commercial premises. Since November 2016, ENER-G has also been known as YLEM Group plc.

SALFORD IN THE TWENTY-FIRST CENTURY

ittle now remains of the old Salford depicted by one of the city's most illustrious adopted sons, the artist L. S. Lowry. The rows of back-to-back terraced houses have long since been demolished along with all but a handful of the corner pubs. Likewise, most of the monolithic textile mills, ironworks and Victorian factories have succumbed to the wrecking ball. Today Salford is a city that would be largely unrecognisable to Lowry and his contemporaries.

Post-war Salford of the 1940s, 1950s and 1960s can now only be seen in the photographic archives held by Salford Museum and Art Gallery at Peel Park, through the exchange of images and recollections on the nostalgia Facebook page 'Memories of Old Whit Lane' and other similar social media sites and, ironically, on Lowry's canvases housed in the dedicated gallery in the ultra-modern Lowry centre at Salford Quays.

Today's Salford, in particular the gleaming waterfront metropolis that has risen phoenix-like from the 'ashes' of the docks, is proving to be a magnet that attracts thousands of new businesses year by year. A high proportion of these are in the global high-tech arena of TV, media, digital communication and cyber security. Others embrace a broad spectrum of business from banking to fashion and travel and tourism.

Slum clearance begins to change the face of Salford. (Author's collection)

New replaces
old – changing
the Salford
skyline. (Author's
collection)

Staff gather for a VIP visit at Mettler-Toledo Safeline. (Courtesy of Mettler-Toledo Safeline)

METTLER-TOLEDO SAFELINE

Back in 1988, four men with a passion for engineering and innovation launched a production company dedicated to detecting traces of metal in food and pharmaceutical production. Safeline started life in a small production space off Frederick Road in Salford, but as the business expanded they moved into larger premises in Montford Road, expanding over time from one to four buildings on the same site.

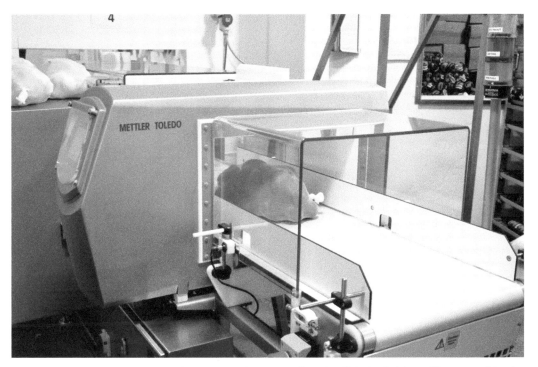

A food product is tested for traces of metal at Mettler-Toledo Safeline. (Courtesy Mettle-Toledo Safeline)

Safeline rapidly became the recognised leader in industrial metal detectors and in 1997 it was acquired by Mettler-Toledo, the leading global manufacturer of precisions instruments with a foothold in thirty-nine countries, 14,200 employees and a £1 billion turnover. Operating as Mettler-Toledo Safeline, the Salford-based company now employs more than 300 staff and manufactures more than 5,000 metal contamination-detection systems a year. In 2016, the company's revenue was £113 million.

As an established leader in the field, Safeline continues to pioneer innovative technology and work with global brand leaders to ensure that the food we eat and the products we use are free from even the tiniest amounts of metal contaminants. The company has twice been awarded the Queen's Awards for Industry and was nominated as the Salford Business of the year in 2012 and 2016.

IN THE STYLE

With no previous experience of the fashion industry but with an innate feel and flair about what young women like to wear, entrepreneur Adam Frisby launched his online In The Style business from his bedroom in 2013. Today, with a global customer base and separate websites in the UK, the USA and Australia, the Salford business has an annual turnover of £30 million – and growing year on year.

In The Style's online range of clothing, shoes and accessories comprises up to 3,000 affordable items including dresses for every occasion, partywear, swimwear, leisurewear, lingerie, knitwear, denim, coats and jackets, all designed in-house at the company's headquarters at Olympic Court,

Entrepreneur Adam Frisby, founder of In The Style. (Courtesy of In The Style)

off Eccles New Road. The Salford premises, with its eighty-five employees, also houses the warehouse, offices and photographic studios. New collections – many created by fashion designers from local colleges – are introduced every few weeks. The garments are made in different parts of the UK and also in the Far East before being returned to the Salford warehouse.

Prior to his successful leap of faith into the fashion industry at the young age of twenty-two, founder Adam Frisby worked in banking, recruitment and, for a time, at Burger King. As the company's chief executive, he maintains an active hands-on day-to-day role.

LATEROOMS.COM

With just six members of staff working from an office in Chapel Street, Salford, LateRooms.com was launched in 1999 as an hotel directory website for properties looking to fill empty rooms at short notice. Initially, there were just 300 hotels listed but the business grew rapidly into a major Online Travel Agency (OTA) now with more than 200,000 properties worldwide, featuring everything from independent B&Bs to luxury spa hotels, budget hostels to serviced apartments.

The company was bought by First Choice Holidays in 2006, merging into the TUI Travel Group in 2007. In 2015, it was bought by Cox & Kings and now has a workforce of more than 200 employees operating under the LateRooms.com brand. Having vacated their former offices in Deva Street, Salford, the company now operates from the high-rise Peninsula Building in Manchester city centre and is a recognised household name in the hotel and travel industry. The founders were brothers Steven, Paul and Tony Walsh and colleague Steve Burton.

Tony Walsh, one of the LateRooms.com founders. (Courtesy of LateRooms.com)

UNIVERSITY OF SALFORD

The University of Salford, like so many of the city's other great institutions and organisations, is rooted in the Industrial Revolution, but it has grown and evolved to meet the changing demands of the digital communication and professional world.

At the height of the city's textile industry and with its access to the global markets provided on its doorstep by the Manchester Ship Canal, the demand for new industrial skills led to the formation of the Pendleton Mechanics' Institute in 1850 and the Salford Working Men's College in 1858, sowing the seeds from which the university would grow.

At the end of the nineteenth century, the institute and college merged to form the Royal Technical Institute, which was officially opened in 1896 by the Duke and Duchess of York – later to become George V and Queen Mary. In 1921, the Institute was renamed the Royal Technical College and it remained as such until 1958 when it was split into two separate organisations: the Royal College of Advanced Technology and the breakaway Peel Park Technical College.

In 1961, the breakaway college became the Peel Park Technical Institute and in 1970 it changed again to the Salford College of Technology; in 1992, it changed for a third time to the University College Salford. In 1967, the Royal College of Advanced Technology became the

Foundation stone laying ceremony for the Royal Technical College, c. 1892. (Courtesy of University of Salford photographic archives)

Typing instruction at the Salford College of Technology, *c.* 1970. (Courtesy of the University of Salford photographic archives)

Icons of the 1960s. The concrete totem sculptures created by William Mitchell for the forecourt of the Allerton Building at Salford Technical College, now part of the university. (Courtesy of the University of Salford photographic archives)

University of Salford when Her Majesty Queen Elizabeth II presented it with the royal charter. In 1996, the two academic bodies merged to create the University of Salford of today – exactly 100 years after the original Royal Technical Institute was established.

The University of Salford today has an increasing global reach with some 21,000 students from all over the world and around 2,500 staff – 1,200 of them being academic staff – working from the original Peel Campus at Peel Park and the Crescent and from the new MediaCityUK Campus at Salford Quays where its academics and students work closely with the BBC and ITV in advancing the frontiers of the communication and broadcasting technologies of the future.

In terms of the world of work, Salford University plays a significant dual role. Along with the city's Salford Royal NHS Foundation Trust, which manages one of the country's top performing

Salford University campus in the 1960s. The original Peel Building (left), the Maxwell Building (right) and the City Museum and Art Gallery (centre). (Courtesy of the Salford Local History Collection)

Salford's elegant Crescent in 1920. The former Salford Royal Hospital is in the background to the left – now converted into apartments. (Courtesy of the University of Salford photographic archives)

The new Salford Royal Hospital in Stott Lane. (Courtesy of the Salford Royal NHS Foundation Trust)

hospitals, Salford Royal, and the City Council it is not only one of the largest employers but also a continuing job creator through the development of spin-off companies. The Salford NHS Trust has some 7,000 employees in all disciplines and departments.

Three spin-off companies, effecting major improvements in the fields of identity access management, aerosol technology and customised TV sound, are worthy of special note.

PROOFID

Starting out as Salford Software in 1988 in the university's computer services department, ProofID is now a global business dedicated to ensuring that companies and individuals have a safe and secure identity by using a single sign-on password when using the Internet or mobile apps. In July 2017, the company merged with a PEGRight Inc. in Colorado, USA, extending their service across the US and Europe with a potential combined market of £18 million. Proof ID has thirty-six members of staff.

SALVALCO ECO-VALVES

Invented by Professor Ghasem Nasr and his team in the School of Computing, Science and Engineering, the Salford Valve Company (Salvalco) Eco-Valves is the 'next generation aerosol technology', using harmless gasses such as nitrogen and carbon dioxide (or, simply, compressed air) as a propellant as an alternative to the more environmentally damaging propane and butane. Patents for the technology were gained in 2008 for various aerosol products including air fresheners, hairsprays, polish and insecticides. In 2014, Salvalco won The Times Higher Award for Outstanding Contribution to Innovation and Technology.

SALSA SOUND

One of the newest spin-offs is Salsa Sound, a company incubated in the university's Acoustic Research Centre, which is currently developing technologies to enhance viewers' experience watching sports broadcasts by tuning into particular sounds – such as the kick of a football and the referee's whistle. Much of the research has been conducted in collaboration with the BBC, Dolby, NBC Universal and the US digital sound specialists, DTS (Dedicated to Sound) and organisations such as Action on Hearing Loss, the Royal National Institute for Blind People and Ofcom. Initially the focus has been on football but over time it will be extended to several other sports.

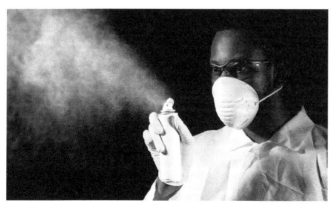

Testing one of the Salvalco Eco-Valve aerosols. (Courtesy of the Salford Valve Company)

PEOPLE AT WORK

JAMES NASMYTH

In the early 1830s, the big shipping companies such as the Great Western Steam Company were experiencing major problems in finding firms that could forge the giant paddlewheel shafts they needed for their vessels. James Nasmyth, a Scottish-born engineer and inventor, came up with the solution in 1842 when he designed and built the world's first steam hammer at his foundry alongside the Bridgewater Canal in Patricroft, Salford.

One of its key features, which overcame the defects of the old tilt-hammer that delivered every blow with the same force, was that the force of each impact could be accurately controlled by the operator. In fact, to show off its capabilities, Nasmyth would demonstrate how it could break an egg placed in a wine glass without breaking the glass but also deliver a blow powerful enough to shake a building.

Nasmyth was also an accomplished draughtsman and some twelve years before inventing the steam hammer he made what he called a 'hasty sketch' of George Stephenson's *Rocket*

James Nasmyth, 1877. (Courtesy of Grace's Guide to British Industrial History)

The Inventor of the Steam Hammer: A Picture taken in 1856
James Nasmyth, the Scottish engineer, with the steel-hammer he invented. It was designed to meet the difficulties of shipbuilders, who could not find firms which would undertake to forge large paddlewheel shafts for steamships. The first steam hammer was built in 1842.

Left: Nasmyth's steam hammer photographed in 1856. (Courtesy of Grace's Guide to British Industrial History)

Below: Nasmyth's sketch of Stephenson's *Rocket*, September 1830. (Courtesy of Grace's Guide to British Industrial History)

NASMYTH'S SKETCH OF THE "ROCKET"

in September 1830 as it stood on the line the day before it made its inaugural run on the Liverpool and Manchester Railway. For Nasmyth, who was there to witness the first run, it was no doubt an event that inspired his own inventive drive.

On a visit to France, with a view to supplying tools to the French arsenal and dockyards, he decided to make a visit the Le Creusot works in the Bourgogne where he was taken on a tour and saw one of his steam hammers in action. He was reported to say on his return: 'There it was, in truth – a thumping child of my brain.' In 1843, Nasmyth went on to invent a pile-driving machine using the same principle. By 1856, his Salford-based company had sold 490 steam hammers across Europe as well as to Russia, India and Australia.

In the same year, Nasmyth – still only forty-eight years old – decided to retire 'to let younger men have their chance', settling down in a house he called Hammerfield at Penshurst in Kent. There he pursued his hobbies of art and astronomy, building a 20-inch reflecting telescope and co-writing *The Moon Considered as a Planet and a Satellite*. Nasmyth built plaster models of the moon's surface based on his observations and made a drawing of a lunar crater. In recognition of his contribution to astronomy, a crater on the moon is named after him. He died, aged eighty-one, in 1890.

FRIEDRICH ENGELS

In 1842, when Salford was at the beating heart of the Industrial Revolution, a young twenty-two-year-old Friedrich Engels came to work at his father's Ermen & Engels Victorian cotton-manufacturing mill in the district of Weaste. En route from his native Germany he met Karl Marx, then the editor of *Rheinische Zeitung*, a publication in which Engels anonymously published articles about the poor working and living conditions of factory workers. They were two events that were to change the whole course of world history.

His father, Friedrich Snr, was a deeply religious man who hoped that by sending him to work in his Salford mill he would abandon his radical aspirations about improving conditions for the working classes, which had smouldered in his mind since his school days in the former industrial Prussian town of Barmen (now in Wuppertal, Germany), but it was in vain. Contrary to his father's hopes, the young Engels saw his time in Salford as an opportunity to witness the conditions for himself firsthand in what would have been an ideal study environment at the ideal time.

The table in the alcove in Chetham's Library reading room where Engels and Marx drafted the principles of Communism. (Courtesy of the author Peter Harris)

The *Engels' Beard* sculpture outside the New Adelphi Building, University of Salford. (Courtesy of the University of Salford Art Collection, photograph by Nick Harrison)

During some two years in Salford, Engels observed the appalling living and working conditions in the slums close to the mill and, with his passion for change reinforced by what he had seen, he submitted three articles to Marx. Back in Germany he collated and edited the articles for his most influential work, *The Conditions of the Working Class in England* which was published in 1845. In it he stressed 'the grim future of capitalism and the industrial age'. In 1887 the book was published in English. The mill, in which Engels was a part-owner until 1869, was demolished in the wake of the M602.

In the summer of 1845, Marx (then living in London) and Engels studied together at a table in an alcove in the reading room of the 350-year-old Chetham's Library, just across the border in Manchester. The thirteen volumes of philosophical thought and political theory they read and absorbed informed and moulded their views, and in 1848 Engels co-authored *The Communist Manifesto* with Marx. Engels later assisted Marx with his research, as well as providing financial help, for his most famous work, *Das Kapital*. A philosopher, social scientist, writer and businessman, Engels died in London in 1895, aged seventy-four.

In September 2012, a 2.3-tonne fibreglass sculpture, *Engels' Beard,* created by contemporary visual artist Jai Redman was erected outside Salford University's New Adelphi Building on the Peel Campus. During his lifetime Engels made it known that he did want any statues or busts erected in his image, but in view of the fact that Redman's artwork focuses on his signature beard as a symbol of his wisdom and learning, he would no doubt have approved of it. It is, in fact, the only tangible image of him anywhere in the city. Rumours that he and Marx drank at the nearby the Crescent public house and drew up *The Communist Manifesto* have been found to be historically inaccurate and nothing more than an urban myth.

WILLIAM WORRALL MAYO

By the time he was in his mid-twenties William Worrall Mayo had a successful tailoring and drapery business in Regent Road, Salford, but it was in the world of medicine on the other side of the world where he would make his name and achieve lasting international recognition.

Attracted by the prospect of a new life in the New World he emigrated to America, along with 248 other passengers, arriving in New York from Liverpool aboard the US-owned packet

William Worrall Mayo in 1868. (Used with permission of the Mayo Foundation for Medical Education and Research. All rights reserved)

vessel the *Oxford* on 22 August 1846. He initially pursued his trade as a tailor and in 1848, along with another tailor, opened a Hall of Fashion in Lafayette, Indiana – but fate would eventually lead him along an entirely different career path.

He became acquainted with a Dr Elizabeth H. Deming who stimulated his interest in medicine, encouraging him to pursue it as a profession and took him on as a student. He graduated in February 1850 and by the 1870s the former Salford tailor was one of the most respected and prominent medical pioneers in Minnesota. His accomplishments extended into the 1890s when he was joined by his two sons in his practice in Rochester – a practice that would evolve to become the internationally renowned Mayo Clinic.

As such, Dr William Worrall Mayo's contribution to the worlds of work, medical research and the health of individuals the world over is inestimable. The Mayo Clinic employs 4,500 physicians and scientists and has a total staff of more than 57,000 at its treatment research and education centres throughout the USA. It treats patients from across the USA and from some 150 countries around the world.

When he was born in 1819, his father, James, was working as a joiner and the family lived on the corner of Oldfield Road and Fleet Street. His mother, Anne Bonsall, was the daughter of a successful farmer and the Worrall side of her family established the Ordsall Dye Works (see section on Salford mills). Dr William Worrall Mayo died in Rochester in 1911, aged ninety-two.

EDWIN ALLIOTT VERDON-ROE

Among mariners, there is a widely held superstition that the albatross is an omen for both good and bad luck. For the 'Ancient Mariner' in Coleridge's epic poem, the shooting of the seabird with a crossbow proved cataclysmic, but for Salford-born merchant seaman Edwin Alliott Verdon-Roe it brought fame, fortune and ultimately the opportunity to conquer the skies.

As he sailed around the globe as an engineer, on vessels operated by the British and South African Royal Mail Co., he observed the majestic albatrosses soaring over the ocean and became increasingly obsessed with the possibility of building a flying machine. It was an obsession that would see him become one of the Britain's great pioneer pilots and aircraft manufacturers and founder, in 1910, of the Avro company.

Born in Patricroft, Eccles, the son of a local doctor, Roe left home when he was only fourteen to travel to Canada to train as a surveyor, but on arrival in British Columbia he

A.V. Roe with his biplane in 1908. (Courtesy of the Avro Heritage Museum)

The green plaque erected by Wandsworth Council in 2011 on the site of the stable workshops where Roe carried out early experiments with his biplane. (Courtesy of photographer William Batchelor)

discovered that there was little demand for surveyors because of a slump in the silver market. So, after spending a year doing various odd jobs, he returned to England where he became an apprentice with the Lancashire & Yorkshire Railway and later joined the Royal Navy.

In 1906, after finishing his naval career, he successfully applied for a job as secretary of the Royal Aero Club where he was offered a job as a draughtsman within a short time. After disagreements about designs and problems with his salary, however, Roe resigned and began working on his own building a series of flying models, one of which won a *Daily Mail* competition with a prize of £75.

Roe used the money to build a full-sized aircraft, the Roe 1 biplane, which was based on his winning design. He tested it at Brooklands in Surrey in 1907–08, recording his first successful flight on 8 June 1908. A year later at Walthamstow Marshes, he became the first Englishman to fly an all-British machine – the Avroplane triplane, now preserved in the London Science Museum.

In 1910, with his brother Humphrey, Roe founded the A. V. Roe Aircraft Co. in Great Ancoats Street, Manchester, selling more than 8,300 of the popular 504 aircraft mainly to the Royal Flying Corps and later to the Royal Air Force. He was knighted in 1929, changing his surname to Verdon-Roe by deed poll, adding the hyphen in honour of his mother. Between 1929 and 1940 he lived at Hamble in Hampshire. He died in hospital in Portsmouth, aged eighty-one, in 1958 and is buried in the churchyard at St Andrew's Church, Hamble.

Above left: A. V. Roe in his study. (Courtesy of the Avro Heritage Museum)

Above right: Statue of James Prescott Joule in Worthington Park, Sale, Greater Manchester, near the house where he died. (Author's collection)

JAMES PRESCOTT JOULE

Physicists the world over associate James Prescott Joule with the unit of energy – the joule – that is named after him, but for connoisseurs of fine ale in a large tract of the North West his name will always be synonymous with Joule's Brewery, which has the sixth oldest beer trademark in the world: the Red Cross.

The son of a wealthy brewer, Joule was born in Salford on Christmas Eve 1818. As a young man he worked in the family brewery, which stood opposite the present Salford railway station until it was sold in 1854; however, it was his fascination in the properties of electricity and electro-chemical reactions that really fired his imagination, pursuing all his initial early research in his spare time.

In 1838, he published his first scientific work in *Annals of Electricity* by William Sturgeon from Whittington, near Carnforth, Lancashire, one of the great evangelists for electricity who had an important influence on Joule's career. In 1850, Joule was elected as a Fellow of the Royal Society and two years later became a recipient of the society's gold medal. He was also an active member of the Manchester Literary and Philosophical Society, serving as a librarian, honorary secretary, vice president and twice as president. Joule died at his home in Sale, Cheshire, in 1889, aged seventy-one. A statue of him can be seen in the local Worthington Park.

Brothers Francis and William Joule, who were born in the mid-1700s, were the first in the family to start brewing ale. William established his reputation for fine ale at the Salford brewery while Francis moved to Stone in Staffordshire, launching the original Joule's Brewery alongside the Trent & Mersey Canal. John Joule, who took over from his father at Stone, cleverly negotiated to take over the Red Cross sign for his ale, which was originally used by Augustine monks who had brewed beer at the priory in Stone since the sixteenth century and who had blessed each new barrel of beer with the Red Cross as a hallmark of its quality. Many years later, the Red Cross was adopted by the international aid organisation with agreement from the brewery that they would not use it on a white background. It is the sixth oldest beer trademark in the world.

The original Joule's Brewery at Stone, Staffordshire. (Courtesy of Joule's Brewery)

Left: Joule's Brewery today at Market Drayton. (Courtesy of Joule's Brewery)

Below: With the red cross trademark on their glass, brewery managing director Steve Nuttall (left) and bank manager Darren Harding enjoy a pint. (Courtesy of Joule's Brewery)

The present – and fourth – Joule's Brewery was opened in 2010 in Market Drayton, just across the border from the old Stone brewery in Staffordshire. It produces around 7,000 barrels of craft ales a year, supplying more than forty pubs in Shropshire, Staffordshire, Cheshire and Wales. Joule's was the first English beer to be exported to the USA and was recorded as stock on the *Titanic* on 10 April 1912.

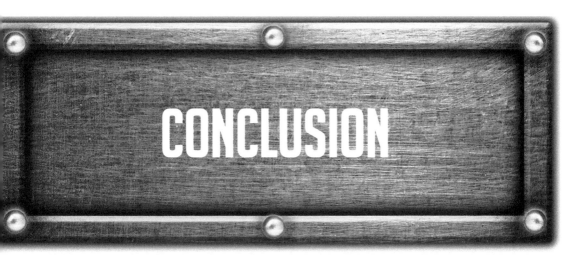

CONCLUSION

Throughout its history Salford has known both good times and bad. It has known great heights and desperate lows, but its people – its workers – have, like those in so many other industrial towns and cities around Britain, always accepted their lot with stoicism coupled with a sense of humour.

Appropriately, this sense of humour is now graphically symbolised by two giant 56-feet-high metal sculptures, *The Skyhooks*, designed by sculptor Brian Fell (a fine arts graduate from the Manchester Polytechnic) and installed at the Quays in neighbouring Trafford in 1995. The massive hooks and chains are a reference to the practical joke requests made by the dockers to greenhorn apprentices 'to go and fetch a sky hook' when, of course, no such thing existed. They are evocative modern works of art that are literally links with the past.

Above left: One of the Skyhooks at the Quays – a symbol of past and present. (Courtesy of the sculpture Brian Fell of Glossop, Derbyshire)

Above right: Sculptor Brian Fell at work. (Courtesy of Brian Fell)

ACKNOWLEDGEMENTS

would like to express my sincere thanks to all the people who willingly and freely provided their time, information and photographs in the preparation of this book. I would especially like to thank the Salford Local History Library and the University of Salford for all their invaluable contributions.

ABOUT THE AUTHOR

eter Harris is a writer and former newspaper journalist who as a young reporter worked for the former *Salford City Reporter* before joining the editorial staff of the *Manchester Evening News*. From the age of seven until his mid-twenties he lived in the Pendleton district of Salford, where his late father was a long-serving family doctor in the city. He and his wife Wendy now live in Sandbach, Cheshire.